Create Successful Walking Tours

Lynne Sturtevant

Copyright © 2019 Lynne Sturtevant

All rights reserved.

ISBN 13:978-1-70-093891-6

CONTENTS

	Introduction	1
1	The Big Picture: Goals, Theme and Structure	7
2	Research	21
3	Designing the Tour	35
4	Staffing the Tour	48
5	Logistics	56
6	Money Matters	66
7	Marketing and Promotion	79
8	Tour Day: What Could Possibly Go Wrong?	96
9	Post-Tour Assessment	116
	About the Author	122

INTRODUCTION

The increasing velocity of societal change, the seemingly endless technological breakthroughs, and our "always connected, always on" lifestyles have many people longing for a simpler, slower time and as a result, the audience for local history tours is growing.

But the old ways of developing and presenting tours no longer work. People's expectations are changing and evolving. They are looking for deeper, more relevant and more interesting experiences. And they are willing to pay for them.

Being aware of this trend is one thing. Knowing how to capitalize on it is a different matter.

That's where **Create Successful Walking Tours** comes in.

Who Is This Book For?

Whether you work in an historic house, for a regional museum, in a Main Street organization, for the Visitors' Bureau or run your own small business, **Create Successful Walking Tours** will help you find appealing ideas for programs, show you how to structure and price your tours properly and market them effectively to the right audiences.

You'll gain competence in critical areas for which you may have had little or no training. This will reduce your stress, increase your confidence and allow you to focus on what you do best – sharing your community's great stories.

You *can* learn to create tours and events that people will gladly pay to attend. You *can* breathe new life into your destination's or attraction's offerings and marketing. You *can* build a successful and rewarding business around local history. This book will show you how.

For Entrepreneurs

Do you dream of firing your boss, ditching the commute and working on something you actually enjoy from the comfort of your own home? Maybe you're a retiree with time on your hands or a stay-at-home parent who'd like to earn some extra cash. Perhaps you're just looking for an interesting side gig. Does the idea of sharing interesting stories about your town appeal to you?

If you said yes, keep reading. This very well may be the fun and profitable business idea you've been searching for.

Starting a local tour business is relatively simple. You don't need office space or a retail location. You don't need employees, inventory, an elaborate business plan or tons of cash. You don't have to quit your regular job.

You can take your time, learn what your community likes, build on your successes and grow at your own pace.

For History Professionals and Local Tourism Folks

Does any of this sound familiar?

Your historic site is hemorrhaging money. Visitor numbers are plummeting. The board expects you to revitalize your attraction without additional funds. You tried a few new programs, but turnout was dismal. You're demoralized, disgusted and out of ideas.

You assumed the small museum hired you because you're an historian and a talented researcher. But you spend your time trying to be a social media expert and an event planner not to mention struggling with an outdated computer system and the ugliest website you've ever seen. You're frustrated and ready to throw in the towel.

You used to love your job managing group tours for the Visitors' Bureau. But the number of buses calling on your town dwindles each year and you cringe every time a tour operator asks, "Why should we come back? Anything new we haven't already seen or done?"

You're the executive director of your town's historic preservation organization. You landed the job because you're a grant writing phenomenon. But the board wants you to design a walking tour of downtown neighborhoods. Even worse, they expect you to guide the darned thing. They might as well ask you to fly to the moon.

Don't despair. Keep reading.

A Custom Design

There are dozens of generic planning guides available, but this is the only one designed specifically for people working in local history and tourism.

It addresses issues such as how to balance the presentation of factual information with entertaining elements, where to find background material, how to effectively use volunteers, how much to charge, and shows you how to do it all while keeping the board, accounting department and various other upper management folks happy. And if you are an entrepreneur running your own history tour operation, it will help you grow your business and add to your bottom line.

The material is based on what I've learned in the trenches over the last several years with my company, Hidden Marietta, creating and running successful – and some not so successful – tours. You and I will be a virtual team. We are going to follow a clear, concrete approach. No fluff. My goal is to help you clarify your thinking and achieve the results you want.

- You'll be following a tested method that takes the guesswork out of planning, promoting and running tours.

- The easy to follow step-by-step instructions keep you from missing critical items.
- This approach allows you to plan your work rationally and avoid last minute emergencies, overload and burnout.
- This book includes templates you can use to create press releases, gift certificates, compensation agreements and more.
- The executive summary section makes preparing meaningful reports for your CEO, CFO, and/or board quick and easy.
- If you supervise inexperienced program developers or want to assign tour planning to another staff member, you can use this book as a training guide.

To get maximum benefit from the material, buy a new notebook or open a fresh folder and take notes as you go along. When you finish, you'll have a record of the timelines, costs, descriptions of problems and unexpected issues, the names and contact information of everyone involved, vendor details, as well as notes on possible improvements and concepts for spinoff events. When the time comes to plan the next tour, pull out your notebook or open your folder. You'll be way ahead of the game.

Creating a tour is like baking a cake. The basic elements of time, place and theme correspond to the flour, eggs, and butter in a recipe. Good cooks, and smart tour designers, know how to tweak recipes to make them better. Adding chocolate transforms a bland cake into a rich, delicious one. Substituting cinnamon, walnuts and raisins yields a totally different concoction. Pouring the batter into cupcake tins creates dozens of little cakes instead of a single big one.

Neither successful tours nor beautiful cakes happen by accident. You exponentially increase your odds of creating a fun and lucrative tour if you think things through in advance. And once you have one successful tour under your belt, putting the next one together will be a piece of cake.

I'll be with you every step of the way from initial idea through the thicket of tour day logistics to post-program assessment. If you run into problems, encounter something that doesn't make sense or just want to kick an idea around, send me an email. My contact information is in the final section. I'll get back to you as soon as I can.

Are you ready? Let's get started.

Chapter 1 – The Big Picture: Goals, Theme and Structure

You're not feeling overwhelmed already, are you? Take a deep breath. As Lewis Carroll wisely advised in **Alice in Wonderland**, it's best to start at the beginning. The first thing we're going to do is establish a foundation and framework for our new tour.

Overall Goal and Defining Success

Understanding why you want to offer the tour helps you stay on course. Do any of these reasons ring a bell?

- To increase visibility for your organization, destination or company
- To make money
- To draw people to a particular part of town
- To showcase or raise awareness of a renovation project
- To provide something fun and educational for the community
- To celebrate your town's history

- To mark a special event
- To learn a new skill
- To enhance your credibility
- Because your boss is making you

Knowing your overall goal allows you to determine whether your tour is successful. If your goal is to earn money and 20 people show up at $20 each, you've just taken in $400. Nice work. However, if your goal is to attract a new audience and all 20 tour participants have attended every program you've offered since the beginning of time, your tour isn't successful at all.

Spend a few minutes thinking about and documenting why you want to offer the tour and what you hope to achieve. You'll find looking back at your notes very interesting later.

Coming Up with a Concept

If you are the kind of person who generates lots of ideas and constantly floats trial balloons, this can be the most exciting and creative phase of tour development. If, on the other hand, you're short on ideas, it can be beyond frustrating.

Even if you're drawing a complete blank, relax. You do not have to come up with an original idea. Combine several elements from the suggestions below then customize the material so that the tour reflects your town's or neighborhood's story.

Use the following words as prompts for brainstorming. Write down at least five things that come to mind as you consider each topic. No editing. Just write. This list is not meant to be all-inclusive. Consider it a jumping off point.

When you've completed the list, read over what you wrote. Did anything interesting surface? How can you relate these topics to your neighborhood or town?

- Architecture
- Ghosts
- Graveyards
- Churches, synagogues, mosques
- Alleys
- Businesses of the past
- Crime and punishment
- Local legends
- Famous or infamous people
- Gardens
- Food
- Drink
- Old taverns and hotels
- Genealogy
- History of sports
- Ethnic heritage
- Pre-colonial history

- 20th century history
- Underground Railroad
- Battles
- Women's rights
- Childhood
- Victoriana
- Archeology

But I Live in Dullsville

Still think there's nothing to talk about in your boring town? Think again. Most people don't look closely at their surroundings, especially if those surroundings are very familiar. When I moved to the small town of Marietta, Ohio, I saw potential for tours and events around every corner. The local folks, especially the lifelong residents, thought I was delusional.

The first program I created was Ghost Trek, an evening walking tour of the historic downtown. Before I offered it to the general public, I took a group of residents on a free test run so I could practice my delivery and make sure the timing worked. Of course, I also wanted to find out whether they liked it. Their reaction was positive but guarded. My favorite comment was, "Well, that was interesting, but who is going to do this? No one wants to take this tour."

As I write this, Ghost Trek is wrapping up its seventh season and more than 7000 people have taken the tour.

Structure and Theme

Just as you must decide whether you're going to make a chocolate or a lemon cake before you start baking, you need to make some preliminary decisions about how your tour will work. Selecting a structure and theme will help you name and promote the tour. It will also help you determine what belongs in the tour and what doesn't.

In some locations, the appropriate structure and theme will be obvious. You'll be able to quickly pull together a tour by focusing on your great old buildings, an historic cemetery or a neighborhood's unusual story.

This may seem counterintuitive, but having an obvious theme is not always an advantage. Obvious can be dull, overdone and predictable. Quirky, weird and interesting are much better. Surprising is the very best element of all.

Here are some possible themes and ways to structure your tour material.

- **Window on the Past** – Drill down on a specific time period. What was happening in downtown Mayfield in 1900? What was the Spring Valley home front like during World War II? How did the Fairview Heights neighborhood change during the Great Depression? What happened in Madison during Prohibition? What role did the residents of Belleville play in the Underground Railroad?

- **Evolution** – If you zoom in on a small area or a single neighborhood, you can broaden the time frame. Two Centuries of Architectural Change in Cherry Hill. Pittsfield Eats: The City Market Through the Decades. Don't miss the opportunity to take any tour that involves food or beverages to the next level by including samples or tastings.

- **Spectacular Events** – Marietta sits at the confluence of two rivers and has been flooded repeatedly over the years plus dozens of wonderful old buildings have been lost to fires. Those disasters inspired a tour called Fire and Water: Agents of Change. Participants travel through downtown looking closely at buildings using old photos to discuss the impact fires and floods have had on the cityscape. What's happened in your town? Has it been plagued by natural disasters such as hurricanes, earthquakes or tornadoes? What about riots, battles or other types of human devastation? Does evidence of any of these events remain?

- **Unifying Topic** – Tie unrelated stops together via a common theme such as ghost stories or mid-century architecture. A unifying topic allows you to stitch disparate elements into a colorful patchwork quilt. Use specific business types as a unifying element such as Brookville's Lost Taverns and Hotels. Tours which cover the seedy side of your town's history – prostitution, murder, smuggling, illegal gambling, gun running, pirates, corruption – are perennial favorites. Name it something like Sunnyvale Vice.

- **Unifying Activity** – Structure your tour around a participant activity such as photography. Offer a Victorian Architecture Photo Walk or hold a photo scavenger hunt where all the clues relate to the area's historic buildings and sites. Upgrade the experience by inviting a professional photographer to come along and give participants tips on how to take great shots of old buildings. Upgrade the price of the tour accordingly. More on this in Chapter 6 on Money Matters.

- **Open House** – If you can get access to the interiors of several buildings, you can set the tour up as an open house. Post a volunteer or staff person at each location to serve as that building's host. The tour participants travel at their own pace from stop to stop where the host tells them about the building and its past. It's critical that you give the hosts good background information on their locations. It really helps if you can find old photos of the various stops.

- **The Combo Platter** – Occasionally a theme never appears. Don't despair. Create a combo platter. Tell one ghost story, cover one big crime, discuss the history of a few buildings via old photos, show ads from businesses that used to be in the area and explore a normally overlooked place like a basement or an alley. The advantage of this approach is you'll get a feel for which stops your audience likes best, information that will come in handy when you design your next tour or event.

- **Crowd Source It** – If you just cannot find a theme, ask people what type of tour they'd like to take, what part of town they're curious about or what aspect of local history they're interested in. Post the question on Facebook or Twitter. Write a blog post about what you're considering and open it to comments. Put a survey in your newsletter or on your website. Ask people you run into casually. Their answers may surprise you. When you know a lot about a topic, it's easy to forget that others may be thrilled with something much simpler than you imagine.

If you do ask people what type of tour they're interested in, make sure you record their answers. Even if their suggestions don't match what you're planning now, they may contain the seeds of future tours or programs.

Field Work

Once you have one or a few potential themes identified, it's time for a scouting mission. Take a stroll through the area or areas you're considering. Try to look at your town as a tourist would, as if you're seeing it for the first time. Snap a lot of pictures.

Walking tours work best when they focus on a small downtown, a few blocks of a large downtown or a specific neighborhood. Your tour should last about 90 minutes, two hours at the absolute outside. We will discuss timing more in Chapter 5 on Logistics. But being aware of the tour's length will help you focus on an appropriately sized area. Not too large; not too small.

You don't need dozens of stops. Fewer interesting or surprising stops are much better than lots of boring ones. Depending on how far apart the stops are, how much you have to say about each one and whether you are going inside anywhere, five or six may be enough.

Inquiring Minds

What do you do if you've only identified a couple of stops or are still searching for a theme? As you're exploring the potential tour area, give your curiosity and imagination a workout. Ask yourself the following questions. Don't worry about the answers yet. We'll talk about how to find those in Chapter 2 on Research.

Is the architecture in the area you're walking through interesting? Interesting and beautiful are not the same thing. Are all the buildings similar? Is there an odd building that seems to be from a different time or that doesn't fit for some other reason?

Are there alleys you can explore? Are there passageways between the buildings? Most people don't bother to spruce up the backs and sides of buildings. Venturing into these less-traveled areas can be like stepping into a time machine. Are there blackened shingles or singed bricks? High water marks? Remnants of train or trolley tracks? Fragments of walls or old foundations? What is hidden in plain sight in your town?

I'm not suggesting you take people where it is dangerous or filthy. But discovering something new, especially in a familiar place, is a fun and interesting adventure. It's like being a detective or an urban archeologist for a little while. People love taking photos in these unexplored areas too.

Are there ghost ads, the painted signs that cling to the brick walls of old buildings, in your area? What products or businesses did they advertise? Does the ad reveal anything about how the building was used?

In some places, a very satisfying tour can be structured around finding, photographing and deciphering ghost ads. If you want to encourage audience engagement – and you should – you can talk about towns that have restored the ads. Is that a good idea or should the old ads be left alone to continue weathering and fading? What do the tour participants think?

The Inside Story

As you make your way through the area on your field trip, notice the businesses currently in the neighborhood. Do you know any of the owners? Could you get access to a normally off-limits area of one of the buildings for the tour? Is there a creepy old basement or a back room where they used to sell bootleg gin?

If you represent a nonprofit, the business owner may be willing to give you access to help your organization or group. If not, you could share a portion of the tour receipts. We'll talk more about how this works in Chapter 6 on Money Matters. Another possibility is to designate the business the tour's official sponsor in exchange for access, in which case you would include their name and logo on all your promotional materials.

If there is an interesting building on the tour route that is normally open to the public, a hotel lobby or a bar for example, arrange to meet with the manager. Determine details such as the date, time and likely number of participants before you have this conversation. Tell the manager what you are planning and ask for permission to bring your group onto the premises. Ask whether he or she knows any stories or quirky tidbits about the building's past. Sponsorship can work in this situation too.

Home Sweet Home

If you are considering a tour of a residential area, approach it the same way you would a commercial one. Ask questions. Was the neighborhood always residential? What about neighborhood businesses like grocery stores, cafes and movie theaters? Are there apartments, schools, churches, synagogues or just houses? Do the houses look like they were built about the same time? Are they the same architectural style or is there a mix? Do they have yards, gardens or big trees? Did anyone famous or infamous ever live in the neighborhood? As you plan the tour route, be mindful of the current residents' privacy and make sure tour participants stay on public sidewalks.

Post-Trip Analysis

Record your thoughts after you return from your scouting mission. What was your overall impression of the area you're considering? List all the potential stops. Don't edit yet. There will be plenty of time for that later. Draw a simple map of the proposed tour route. Are there any issues regarding sidewalks, parking, safety, etc.? What questions do you have about the area?

If you still feel unsettled, consider venturing a little further afield. Find a walking tour in another part of town or a neighboring town. Be a tourist, travel incognito and participate in that tour. The people offering the tour don't need to know why you're there or what you're up to. Keep an open mind and see what you can pick up. Sometimes learning what doesn't work is just as valuable as learning what does.

The Name Game

Start jotting down possible names for your tour. It should grab people's attention and pique their curiosity. The tour's name is like a newspaper headline. Call it something like Secret San Jose or The Wilmington History Mystery Walk. If you're working on a combo platter, call it something like The Pleasantville History Sampler. You'll be using the title in promotional pieces so don't make it too long. But above all, please make it interesting.

Even if you still don't know what your theme is, don't give up. Some cakes take longer to bake than others. The ideal structure, theme and even the perfect name often emerge during the research phase, which is what we will turn to next.

Chapter 2 – Research

Once you've identified a potential area for your tour, it's time to hit the library, historical society, courthouse and Internet to see what you can discover about the neighborhood.

Down the Rabbit Hole

Research can be mesmerizing and it's easy to go off on tangents. You need factual information, of course. But you also need background and context, the kind of material sportscasters call color commentary. Remember, you are not writing a thesis. Don't lose your focus. The rabbit hole is a cozy, comfortable and fascinating place where it's easy to lose track of time. Keep one eye on the clock and don't stay too long.

You've Got a Friend

There is so much information available, figuring out where and how to start can be overwhelming. You can save yourself a lot of time and trouble by talking to your local librarian. Good librarians don't just know what's in their own collections; they know what's available online and what you may find at other facilities in your community.

Explain what you're doing. Say something like, "I'm developing an historic walking tour and need some background information. The tour is going to cover the section of downtown from Main to Palmer Street between First and Fourth Avenues. I'm interested in the period from 1900 to 1950. I basically want to chronicle how it changed over those 50 years. I want to know what businesses were there. Were there hotels, bars, department stores, pool halls or churches? Were there any major crimes, fires or other spectacular events? I'm also looking for stories about interesting or quirky people who lived or worked in the neighborhood. And I'd love to see old pictures."

Questions to keep in mind include:
- Was the area used in a different way than it is now?
- Was it ever residential?
- If it's residential now, was it always that way?

Offline Sources

The location of offline material will vary by town and state. The items you need may be in a public library, a private college or university library, state or local historical society archives or within city or county departments.

- **Local Histories** — These come in lots of different formats including books, pamphlets, high school research papers and college theses. They range from the very detailed to the rudimentary. They all contain information. If you can find one written close to the time period you're going to cover on your tour, congratulations. You may have hit the jackpot.

- **Board of Trade or Chamber of Commerce Publications** — These were quite popular from the late 1800s into the mid-20th century. They are frequently overlooked because most are little more than glorified marketing documents. Nevertheless, they usually contain good descriptions of commercial districts and the businesses within them in addition to the pictures of people shaking hands.

- **Programs from Special Events** — Did your town have a big celebration on its 100th birthday or receive some kind of crazy award or designation? There may be an official program commemorating that event and it may contain lesser known tidbits about the town's past.

- **Topical Files** — Over the last century or so librarians all over the country have dutifully clipped and filed newspaper articles about local people, businesses, buildings, fires, freak weather events, murders, schools, etc. These humble clipping folders are gold mines of fascinating information.

They often contain the human-interest stories that bring your tour to life.

When I was creating Ghost Trek, I went to the library looking for information. The librarian opened a squeaky metal file cabinet and pulled out an old folder full of crumbly, yellow newspaper clippings. For decades around Halloween, the local newspaper had run a filler article about a haunted house, spooky local legend or ghost story and the librarians had carefully clipped and filed each one. There were only five or six stories that were recycled over and over. However, as I flipped through the file, I knew I had just been handed enough material for a dynamite tour.

Another librarian told me he began a clipping file on multiple births after his own twin sons were born. He continued it for about ten years before moving on to something else. You never know what you're going to find in clipping files and investigating them is an excellent way to spend a couple of hours.

- **Scrapbooks** – Whereas the topical files described above are maintained by librarians, scrapbooks are created by private individuals and sometimes end up in libraries and local historical societies. They reflect someone's personal interests. However, that doesn't mean they don't contain material you would find helpful. It's worth checking.

- **City Directories** – These were produced from the 19th century until the early 20th century when they were replaced by phonebooks. They are essentially listings of the residents and businesses in town along with their addresses and phone numbers, if they had them. Often the lists are displayed twice; once alphabetically and then by address, which can be very helpful. In most places the directories were not published every year, but rather came out every five – ten years. Comparing directories over time can help you plot a business's or neighborhood's growth or demise.

- **Phonebooks Including the Yellow Pages** – For tour creation purposes, the Yellow Pages are much more interesting than the White Pages, which is an alphabetical list of residential and business names, addresses and phone numbers. The Yellow Pages contain business listings and ads. An ad can tell you a lot about a company. Some are quite elaborate and include pictures and maps.

- **Individual Records and Indexes** – This category includes a huge number of sources such as census records, court records, naturalization records, obituary indexes, birth indexes, marriage indexes, divorce indexes, military records, wills and cemetery indexes. These records are stored in various places such as Health Departments and Courthouses. More and more jurisdictions are making these documents available online.

- **Land and Property Records** – These include deeds, property sales and transfers, tax records, etc. There can be useful information in these documents especially if you are interested in very early time periods. Going through this material can get technical, however. You may need to hire an assistant or try to find the answers to your questions some other way. If you get stuck, talk to the folks at the library.

- **Newspapers** — Old local newspapers are certainly one of the best sources of information about your town. Unfortunately, using them and finding relevant information can be a bit tricky. In many places old newspapers are stored on microfiche or microfilm. The staff at the library will show you how to operate the special equipment you need to view this material.

The challenge is most of the content is not indexed and that which is indexed is not organized or categorized consistently. You will probably have to sort through a lot of irrelevant material. If you can zero in on an individual or business name, you may be able to use a search function. Don't expect quick and easy results, though. This is nothing like online research.

Don't overlook newspaper ads. Just like Yellow Pages ads, they say a lot about a business. They capture moments in time. Another useful feature that appears in many newspapers is the "One Hundred Years Ago Today" column or something similar. It's usually filler material pulled from the paper's archives. If your paper includes this type of information, spend some time reading through as many of these columns as you can. A lot of it is dull, reports of club meetings, etc. But some of the snippets are beyond bizarre and will be perfect additions to your tour.

Many big city newspaper archives are accessible online. More and more small-town papers are being added each year. It's a slow process, however.

Online Research

Spending time online researching your town's past will yield a startling amount of information. If you limit your search to what you find through Google, Yahoo or other search engines, however, you will see only a fraction of what's available.

Many of the best online sources are behind paywalls, only accessible to those with paid subscriptions. What's a tour designer to do? Once again, the library comes to the rescue.

Go to your public library's website and look for something like "Electronic Resources." It will probably be in the reference section. You'll find a list of the premium services and databases the library subscribes to on behalf of its customers. All you need to gain access is your library card or membership number. Your librarian will gladly explain how to use these services.

Here are a few examples of premium sources I can access through my small-town library in Ohio. There are many more and the list is ever expanding.

- **Biography Reference Bank** – Biographies, obituaries and photographs of thousands of individuals both living and deceased. Biographies Plus Illustrated contains the full text of the articles from more than 100 volumes of biographical reference books published by H. W. Wilson, plus thousands of profiles licensed from other respected publishers; updated monthly.

- **Explore Ohio** – OPLIN's ever-expanding directory of Ohio-specific websites and links.
- **Heritage Quest Online** – U.S. Census from 1790-1930, Revolutionary War Pension Records & Bounty-Land Warrant Application files, Freedman's Bank Records, and U.S. Serial Set.
- **Ohio History Central Online Encyclopedia** – An evolving, dynamic online encyclopedia from the Ohio Historical Society. Find information, images, timelines, maps, and documents about Ohio's history, geography, geology, animals, and American Indian populations.
- **Ohio Memory Online Scrapbook** – Project to bring together digital versions of historical collections from more than 330 archives, historical societies, libraries, and museums. Search or browse more than 26,000 primary sources dating from prehistory to the present. Take the Ohio Memory Challenge. Read essays about Ohio topics. Create your own scrapbook.
- **World Book Encyclopedia** – Resources include encyclopedic content, e-books, multimedia, a vast collection of primary source documents, and a wealth of research tools that allow users to customize and save their work.
- **America's Newspapers** – Search current and archived editions of Ohio newspapers. Covers issues, events, people, government, sports and more with this collection of full-text newspapers. Includes staff-written

articles, obituaries, editorials, announcements, real estate and other sections.

- **Access Newspaper Archive** – Searchable newspaper pages, dating as far back as the 1700s.

Treasure Maps

An historical street map of the area you are planning to tour can be an amazing source of detailed information. Some of them are truly treasure maps. The good news is they are relatively easy to find.

- **Sanborn Maps** – These incredibly detailed street plans, also known as Sanborn Fire Insurance Maps, were created for more than 12,000 towns and cities between 1867 and 2007. As their name implies, the maps were designed to help insurance companies assess fire liability. The maps zero in on specific blocks. They show each building's outline, address and use. The names of public buildings, churches, businesses and schools are included. The maps even show the location and course of natural features such as creeks as well as railroad tracks, canals, fire hydrants, gas mains and much, much more. You may find that Sanborn Maps were not created for your town, your neighborhood or for the time period you're researching. To further complicate matters, over the years, many were lost to fires, floods and other less dramatic forms of destruction such as insect damage. Sanborn Maps exist both in hardcopy and digital formats and are generally available through the library. I sincerely hope you can use them in your research. They will make your task much easier.

- **Historic Map Works** – This company describes itself as "The world's largest online historical map resource." You may browse to your heart's content. However, there is a fee to download or print material from the site. Again, check with your library. They may have a premium subscription for their patrons, or they may know of a better source for your city or town.

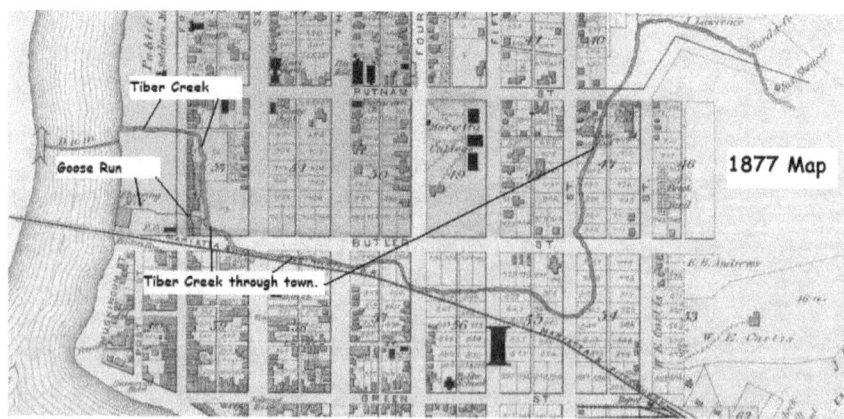

- **Atlases** — There are many other types of maps that can help you understand your area's story. Some old atlases contain almost as much information as Sanborn Maps. Be on the lookout for town plans, property tax maps and population density charts. If a freeway was built through your town at some point, there may be maps of the neighborhoods prior to the road construction project. You'll find all these maps in the usual places: libraries and historical societies.

Photographs

It's likely you will come across vintage images in the course of your research. You'll find them in books, pamphlets, newspapers, photo albums, family collections and scattered over the web. Thousands of vintage pictures have been digitized and uploaded to social media platforms like Facebook, Twitter and Pinterest. Studying old images of the area you'll be touring gives you insights that you can't get from reading documents or even from listening to spoken descriptions. Vintage images can also take your marketing materials to the next level and really stimulate interest in your tour.

Finding pictures is easy. The question is whether you can use them.

Photographs, just like written works, are protected by copyrights. Just because you find an image online, as a result of a Google search, for example, does not mean the image is in the public domain. It only means Google thinks it matches what you're looking for. You also do not hold the copyright to an image because you have physical possession of the negative or print.

The photographer is the copyright holder, even if that person is deceased.

Happily, many of the pictures we want to use to promote historic tours are copyright free due to their age. All photographs published in the United States before 1923 are in the public domain, which means they are no longer copyrighted. Works published after 1922, but before 1978 are protected for 95 years from the date of publication. If the work was created, but not published, before 1978, the copyright lasts for the life of the photographer plus 70 years.

Copyright laws vary by country. If you are outside the United States, you need to determine the rules for your location. If you have questions or concerns about whether a specific item is copyrighted, contact an attorney. Copyright infringements can lead to hefty fines as well as criminal charges.

If you cannot locate any old photos, you are probably looking in the wrong place. Talk to your librarian or contact the folks at the historical society.

Even if you do find a good cache of pictures, consider putting out a call for photos on social media. Tell people what you're looking for. Ask them to check the attic and the old family albums and to post whatever they find to your Facebook page. They may turn up some interesting shots. This will also start building buzz for the tour. We'll talk about incorporating vintage images into your marketing and collateral materials in Chapter 7 on Marketing and Promotion.

Sources

Enter enough information in your folder or notebook so that you – or someone else – can find your sources again later. If you have made copies of anything or have hard copy notes, scan and/or file them.

Lingering Questions

At the end of your research it's OK to have a few unanswered questions. Use them to your advantage. Add them to the tour and let the participants mull them over. This encourages audience engagement and participation.

- We don't really know when all the windows in this old building were bricked up or why it was done. Anyone have any ideas?
- There was supposedly a double murder in this building during the 1930s when it was the Lancaster Arms Hotel. The story always comes up when we talk to older residents. They say their parents told them about it, but we can't seem to find any documentation. What have you heard?

- This is a mystery picture. It looks like it was taken in this block but where was the photographer standing? What are we looking at? Is this even Cambridge?

I hope you have a file full of notes, pictures and maps. It's time to pull it all together and make sense out of the chaos.

Chapter 3 – Designing the Tour

This is where all the bits and pieces come together. It's time to mold your research, the faded pictures of the old neighborhood, maps, newspaper clippings and stories into a coherent whole, a tour experience people will love.

Description

Write a general description of the tour, just a few sentences. Include the theme, what it covers, what people will get out of it. Don't stress over this. You can fine-tune it as you go along. Don't skip this step. We'll revisit this when we do the post-tour assessment. Add it to your folder or notebook. You will probably find looking back at what you wrote quite interesting later.

Sequencing – Plotting Your Course

Take a first pass at laying out the itinerary. I say a first pass because you won't know whether you've nailed it until you walk the route with an actual group. List the stops then rank them in order of most to least interesting. If you haven't done so already, draw a little map.

Remember, you can always change the sequence of stops. In fact, sometimes you must because of unanticipated obstacles like road closures. There's more on those kinds of issues in Chapter 8 – Tour Day: What Could Possibly Go Wrong?

It's critical that the tour have a big opening and a big finish. Look at your stops. Some are undoubtedly more interesting than others. Can you alternate the exciting ones and the stops that are more routine? Think about how long you'll be at each location. Can you balance short and long stops?

The route needs to be logical. It does not, however, have to follow a linear path. I like to construct tours so that they end near where they started. The route is basically a big circle. You can go up one side of the street and come back down the other or take a shortcut through an alley. Do what's efficient with a minimum of backtracking.

Are there long stretches between any stops? I once went on a tour that included what felt like an endless march past generic office buildings and empty parking lots. The guide trudged silently along about half a block ahead of the group. We had no idea where we were going or how long it would be until we reached the next stop. I was not familiar with the area. If I had known how to get back to my car, I would have left the tour.

Sometimes there's no way around it. You must include a long walk through an uninteresting area because the next stop is worth it. Make sure it really is. And remember, you know the stop makes the walk worthwhile, but your customers don't. Say something like, "It's going to take us a few minutes to get to the old Masonic Temple, but it's spectacular and we're going inside." Then, of course, it must actually be spectacular.

The group is going to have to walk back from that great stop too. If the distant stop really is that special, maybe you should build a separate tour around that location, its story and its neighbors. It's something to consider.

If you decide to stick with the distant stop, you need to break up the long walking segment. Figure out where you can add an intermediate stop. Are there benches along the way or a low wall people can sit on for a few minutes? If there really isn't anything to look at or a logical place to stop, just pick a spot that is about halfway. Then tell a story.

Go back to the library or historical society or get online and find something interesting. Is there a weird anecdote about the people who founded the town? Do you have pictures or the names of the businesses that used to be in the neighborhood? Can you talk about the freak snowstorm or the summer it never rained? If you're in the midst of a sea of parking lots, talk about what was there before. When were the buildings torn down? Why? Although your primary goal is to fill time and give people a break, you do not have permission to be boring.

When you think you've got the route figured out, take another field trip. Go back to the neighborhood. Walk the route from start to finish. See how it feels. Time it. Tweak the route if you need to then start writing the scripts for each stop.

Scripting the Stops

I used to be uncomfortable with the idea of scripting tours. I was afraid it would lead to the listless, disengaged presentations we've all endured at various historic attractions. I worried that asking guides to follow scripts would stifle improvisation, force them to conceal their personalities and turn interesting presenters into dull ones. I was wrong.

I used to give guides a bullet point outline. I'd go over it with them, fill in all the juicy details and ask them if they had any questions. I expected them to take it from there because that's how I like to work. That was not a reasonable expectation. Giving guides scripts helps them do better jobs. They can focus on their delivery rather than worrying about what they are going to say next.

Start scripting the stops. Begin with bullet points. List the facts, name of the stop, the reason it's interesting or important, whether you have pictures or old ads. What is each stop's story? Some of this material will be deleted as you develop the script. Don't worry about that now. Just get it all down. Here's an example of a first cut.

Stop: Unitarian Church

- Started in 1855, completed in 1857
- Nahum Ward, died 1860, talk about his funeral, the thunderstorm and flood
- Legend of the freed slave building the wooden staircase, a masterpiece
- The singing ghost in the choir
- People uneasy in choir loft alone, coldness, strangeness
- Sacred places and the power of place

Outlines vs Scripts

Here's a comparison of an outline and a script. The material is from Ghost Trek. The stop includes two theaters, the Colony and the Mid-Ohio Valley Players known as the MOVP. They are across the street from each other and both are supposedly haunted.

Outline

- MOVP built in 1914 for vaudeville, movies, live performances
- Many people have felt a presence in the MOVP. Cold breeze, the eerie not alone feeling, taps on shoulders, shadows in the projection booth
- There is also a presence in the Colony, built in 1919.

- People think the same ghost, Mr. Shea, is in both theaters. He owned a string of small-town theaters in the 1920s including the MOVP and the Colony.
- There is a tunnel beneath the street that connects the theaters.
- Now the Colony is under construction.

Script

- This used to be the heart of Marietta's thriving theater district. Across the street is the MOVP Theater, a vaudeville house built in 1914. It's now the home of our community players.
- We're standing in front of the Colony. It opened in 1919. Both theaters had live performances and movies.
- At one point these theaters were physically connected. There is a tunnel under the street that actors used to travel unseen between the two buildings. The fire department went through the tunnel a few years ago and inspected it. After the inspection, it was sealed, bricked up. It's right beneath where we are standing at this very moment.
- There's another thing these two theaters have in common. They're both haunted. And in what has to be one of the most peculiar stories in a town filled with odd stories, they're haunted by the same ghost. His name is Mr. Shea.
- Mr. Shea's office was right up there in the MOVP. We know he used the tunnel to travel between the two buildings. He might still be using it.
- For decades people have seen his ghost in both buildings. In the MOVP he sits in the back row during performances

and sometimes paces back and forth in the projection booth. Over here, he sits in the balcony or walks the perimeter of the main floor. He's tall and he wears a brown derby hat.
- The Colony closed in 1985 and sat empty for many years. However, it is being renovated and brought back to its former glory. Sometimes remodeling projects in old empty buildings stir up dormant paranormal energy. That seems to be the case here. Mr. Shea sightings are on the rise.
- And guess what? I have the keys. We're going in.
- There's no electricity. It's pitch black in here. If you have a flashlight or a light in your phone, turn it on. We have some flashlights inside too. Get ready to take pictures. This place is awesome!

Managing Your Material

For a brand-new tour, I recommend you write out the entire itinerary including every stop, even if you are the guide and the only one who will be using the script. By writing it all out, you'll understand the material better and be more likely to structure the itinerary and the stories effectively.

Some people feel compelled to jam every name, date and tidbit of information into their tour presentation. This is a huge mistake. This is not a classroom lecture. No one standing outside and listening is going to pick up the finer points. You will frustrate and bore your audience if you wander too far into the weeds. Scripting will help you stay on track.

Scripting also helps guides stay on schedule. Have you ever been on a tour that ran way over time? Inexperienced guides sometimes think this is a plus. They want to give the participants all the information they possibly can. This is not the way customers view it, however. If the tour was advertised as lasting 90 minutes and you are at the two-hour point, stop talking. You're not giving people more value for their money. You're disrespecting their time.

Beginnings, Middles and Ends

The tour's beginning and end are the portions that will benefit the most from a strong script. This will help you get started smoothly and know when to stop talking, which is harder than it sounds. Your best stop, the highpoint of the tour, should be carefully scripted as well, especially if it includes an element of surprise.

Opening Strong

"Hello everyone! Welcome to Fire and Water: Agents of Change. We're really glad you're here. My name is Lynne. This is my partner Megan. We'll be your guides today.

"We have a handout for you. It's a packet of vintage pictures of the places we'll be visiting. If you didn't get one, raise your hand and Megan will fix you up. I see a lot of you have cameras. That's fantastic! There are no restrictions on photography. Take as many pictures as you want. If you get a great shot, we'll post it on Facebook later.

"We've got a large group so let's try to stay together. If you can't hear me, wave, give me some other signal or tell Megan and I'll turn up the volume on the mic.

"Questions? Everybody good? OK! Let's get started. Our first stop is just down the street. We're going to talk about the most catastrophic fire in Marietta history."

This kind of opening accomplishes several things. By welcoming people and introducing yourself, you begin to establish a connection. You let people know they're in the right place. A friendly yet confident tone lets them know they're in good hands. They can relax and enjoy the tour.

The Big Reveal

The best stop on Ghost Trek and our big finale – which is not an accident – is outside an old building that used to be a Sanitarium. Most local people have forgotten about the building's history and, of course, out-of-town folks are completely unaware of its creepy past. There is a large faded sign painted on the building: Chronic Diseases Sanitarium. The letters are almost invisible and no one notices them until the guide points them out.

This is how the stop is supposed to proceed. The group arrives and the guide says, "This building opened in 1900. It has always had retail outlets on the ground floor. There used to be apartments in the upper two floors. The apartments are empty now. The landlord had a hard time keeping them rented. Tenants heard things, the sounds of people weeping and occasional screams. People often felt uneasy in the building, uncomfortable and sort of queasy. No one could figure out what was going on. That's because they didn't come out here, stand where we're standing, and take a good hard look at the building."

The guide points to the upper floors. Everyone looks up. "Can you see the barest remains of letters above the third-floor windows?" People squint, stare and then they see them. The guide waits a minute or so then literally spells it out. "C-H-R-O-N-I-C. Chronic. Look to the right a little. The next word is Diseases." At this point people are gasping and cameras are going off left and right. "Now look under the third-floor fire escape. Do you see the letters? It's the Sanitarium."

People love this stop because of the surprise factor and the way the information is slowly revealed. They're totally involved in what's happening, guessing and figuring things out as the guide goes through the letters. We explain a little more about the facility, the type of patients they served, etc. But we are basically at the end of the tour. This is the stop people talk about, the one they remember. Unless the guide blows it.

I tagged along one night and accompanied our longest serving guide on her ghostly rounds. When we arrived at the final stop, the first words out of her mouth were, "This place used to be a Sanitarium." This was the equivalent of telling a joke by starting with the punchline. People were mildly interested in the story, but it basically bombed and then everyone went home. Ho hum.

This would never have happened if I had scripted the stop.

Clear Finish

As odd as this may sound, you need to let people know when the tour is over. This is the time to thank everyone once again. Take a moment to let them know how to stay in touch with you or your organization. If you have other programs, tell them.

For example, we collaborate with an historic house and offer a Victorian Funeral program each October. We make a point of mentioning this at the end of Ghost Trek starting in late September. Don't go on and on. Just let people know there are other things coming up that they may be interested in. If they have questions, they'll ask.

You must accompany people back to where the tour started. Do not assume they know the way. Do not leave them in an unfamiliar place.

"This is the end of the tour. We enjoyed spending the evening with you and we hope you had a good time. If you want to keep up to date on our tours and special programs – we are coming up with new things all the time – join us on the Hidden Marietta Facebook page. If you'd like to post any of the pictures you took tonight on our page, we'd love that! You can also sign up for our free newsletter at our website, HiddenMarietta.com.

"Megan and I are going to walk back to the fountain where we started. If your car is up here, or you want to revisit some of the stops or duck into one of the bars, please go right ahead. Enjoy! If you're going to walk with us, let's go! Thanks everyone!"

Continuity

Add simple transitions to your script. Tours can feel choppy. The effective use of transitions creates a sense of continuity and really elevates the experience. Giving people a hint as to what's coming up piques their curiosity and keeps them engaged while you're walking to the next stop.

- "Anyone staying at the Lafayette Hotel? Wow. Boy do I have some stories to tell you. Let's go. It's our next stop."
- "Let's go down this alley. It's like walking back in time."
- "I've mentioned floods a couple of times this afternoon. Let's go into the next block and look at some flood markers. You're not going to believe how deep the water was."

Scripts for Hosts

If your tour is an open house-style event, with stationary hosts and participants traveling from location to location, scripts are still a good idea. The first year we offered our Hidden Places, Secret Spaces tour, I gave the building hosts bullet point outlines. The hosts did not have enough background information and did not fully engage with the visitors in some cases.

The following year I scripted each stop and gave the volunteers lots of historic photos. This helped them understand and explain the significance of the sites. Sharing the photos also helped them make the past real for the guests. Audience and volunteer satisfaction went through the roof.

Your tour is really starting to take shape. Nice work! Let's talk about who is going to conduct it. Staffing is up next.

Chapter 4 - Staffing the Tour

Guides make or break tours. Lousy guides come in many forms: dull guides; exhausted guides; unfriendly, exasperated, angry or put upon guides; guides people can't hear; those who talk over visitors' heads or who oversimplify; windbags who won't shut up; narcissists; guides who walk too fast or too slow; and those who clearly, desperately wish they were somewhere else. I bet you've encountered at least a few of these folks. It doesn't matter how good the material is. If the guide is poor, the tour will bomb.

On the other hand, an enthusiastic, well-prepared, engaging guide can transform routine material into something special and create an experience people recommend to their friends.

Guides and Helpers

The first thing you must decide is how many guides you need. If you expect a small group, 10 or 15 people for example, one guide will be fine. I have been the sole guide many, many times and even with very large groups have not had a problem.

However, there is something to be said for having a partner who serves as a helper. This is especially true when you are just starting out. It also makes sense to recruit a helper if you anticipate a large turnout or you're not sure how many people will show up. Your helper can bring up the rear, make sure no one falls behind and let you know if people can't hear.

Your helper can also help check people into the tour. Depending on how you have set up reservations, ticketing and payments – all of which is covered in detail in Chapter 5 on Logistics – you may have people with tickets or people with cash who need change. This can get confusing.

People sometimes arrive late and want to join the tour after it's started. If you have a helper, he or she can handle these situations while you continue with the program. Your helper can also distribute handouts if you are using them.

Another benefit of having a helper is he or she can take photos of the tour in progress. You can feature the pictures on your website, post them on social media and use them in future promotions.

The helper role is great for people training to be guides. They get a realistic look at what they are getting themselves into.

Finding Help

If you need to recruit guides or other people to help in various ways, you have a few options.

- **Paid Staff** – If you work for an organization that has employees and the tour is being offered or sponsored by your organization, maybe staff can be assigned to work on the tour as part of their routine duties. You can also pay a guide or helper out of the proceeds from the tour. Just be very clear up front what percentage you're offering and how it will be computed. More about this below and in Chapter 6 on Money Matters.

- **Volunteers** – If you are working for or with an organization that has a volunteer base such as a Main Street group, historical society or merchants' association and the tour benefits the organization in some way, you may be able to approach their volunteers for help. Depending on what role you expect volunteers to play, other possibilities include community theater groups and college and high school drama or service clubs. Volunteers often do not show up or cancel at the last minute. Be sure to recruit extra volunteers.

- **Friends and Family** – As a last resort, draft a buddy to help you. Bribe your nephew with a crisp $20 or put out a call for help disguised as an invitation to participate in something fun on social media.

Duties and Responsibilities

You don't need to hire an attorney to draw up a contract for your guides and helpers. You must, however, be crystal clear about what their duties and responsibilities are. Keep it as simple as you can and put it in writing.

Compensating Guides and Helpers

If your guides and helpers are not employees of your organization or volunteers, you have a couple of options regarding compensation. You can offer them a portion of the tour's receipts, a flat fee or a combination.

I give the Ghost Trek guides a choice. They can receive a guaranteed $35 per night even if no one shows up or they can opt for 1/3 of the night's receipts. Ghost Trek has been running for several years and we have attendance figures so I can show them exactly how this will work and how much they are likely to earn. They must choose their compensation plan at the beginning of the tour season. No switching mid-stream.

People almost always make more money with the 1/3 share. Most freelancers recognize that right away and choose that option. Some folks, however, are risk-adverse and want the guarantee. Helpers receive a flat fee of $20.

Guides and helpers, especially the good ones, will receive tips. Our policy is that any tips are theirs to keep. If your tour is being offered by your company or an umbrella nonprofit of some sort, I highly recommend you discuss the issue of tips with HR or your boss. That way everyone will know how to handle the situation when it comes up, which it will.

Two of our veteran guides cooked up an interesting variation on this compensation scheme. They work as a team and take turns speaking at alternate stops. While one is presenting, the other serves as the helper. This gives each of them a rest between speaking stops and it gives the tour participants some variety. At the end of the evening, they compute the guide amount at 1/3, add the helper's $20, then split the total in half. It costs Hidden Marietta the exact same amount and it makes them happy.

Sample Guides and Helpers Agreement

This is the agreement we use for Ghost Trek guides and helpers. Feel free to adapt it to your circumstances.

- **The Sign** – Place the sign as early as possible (shoot for around 10am) at the tour meeting place each day that tours will be offered. Remove the sign at the end of the evening.

- **Hours** – Arrive at the tour meeting place at least 30 minutes prior to the scheduled start time. If no one shows up, stay until 10 minutes past the scheduled start time to make sure there are no stragglers.

- **Bad Weather** – Arrive at the tour meeting place at least 30 minutes prior to the scheduled start time. You are responsible for deciding whether the tour will operate. Use your best judgment. If you decide to cancel the tour, remain onsite until 10 minutes past the scheduled start time to inform customers of the cancelation.

- **Turn Out** – Keep track of the number of people broken down between adults and children for each session.

- **Customer Money** – Collect the admissions and make change for customers. I will provide $100 in cash for change. No checks or credit cards. Adults $15. Kids 12 and under $10. Babies and toddlers are free.
- **Itinerary** – Conduct the tour according to our scripts.
- **Guide Compensation** – The guide receives 1/3 of the night's receipts (or $35 if that was the option selected). Tips are yours.
- **Helper Compensation** – For groups of less than 10 the guide will decide whether the helper is needed. When the helper works, he or she will receive $20. The helper's pay is deducted from the company's 2/3, not from the guide's portion. Tips are yours.
- **Comps** – We occasionally have customers with gift certificates. Staff people from the Visitors' Bureau and hotels are always free. Include these people in your attendance counts and compute your pay as if they paid full price.
- **Taxes** – Guides and helpers are not employees of Hidden Marietta. You are independent contractors. You are responsible for your own taxes.

Helping Guides Succeed

Successful guides are enthusiastic, energetic, open and friendly. They are also flexible. Unexpected things happen on tours. Buildings that are supposed to be open are locked. Storms roll in out of nowhere. Streets are closed. Equipment fails. Resourcefulness and a sense of humor are invaluable assets.

We'll delve more into how to deal with the sundry crazy problems that can and do pop up in Chapter 8 on Tour Day: What Could Possibly Go Wrong?

The best gift you can give a guide, even if you're the guide and you're giving the gift to yourself, is a detailed script and schedule of a well-thought out, carefully planned and well-researched tour itinerary.

The fewer things left to chance, the higher the likelihood of a successful tour. Having things spelled out in advance also takes a lot of pressure off the guides and lets them focus on what they do best.

How to Use Scripts and Notes

Conducting a tour is like performing in a play and giving a speech rolled into one. It's intimidating until you get used to it. The biggest fear people have is forgetting their material. Having the script helps reduce the anxiety level.

Having a script also frees guides from worrying about what to say next. When the material is taken care of, they can focus on the audience and on their delivery. Because they tend to be more relaxed with a script, their personalities come through loud and clear. There are plenty of opportunities for improvisation, to throw in that interesting snippet of historical gossip.

Good guides are prepared. This does not mean the guides must memorize every scintilla of information about each tour stop. Some tours are offered over and over and guides will naturally memorize the material through repetition. Other programs are offered one time or just once or twice a year. In these cases, the guides don't work with the material often enough to memorize it.

It's perfectly fine for guides to check their scripts to make sure they are giving accurate information. Tour participants do not mind if you reach into your pocket and pull out an index card. Tell them what you're doing. Say something like, "Let me check my notes. I want to make sure I'm giving you the correct date." And if you draw a complete blank or lose your train of thought, which will probably happen at some point, having a security blanket in the form of your script is a major plus. If you make a mistake, correct it and move on.

Above all, remember, this is not about you and how much you know about the subject. It's about the story you're telling and it's about the participants. Keep that in mind and you'll do fine.

Let's turn to the logistical and administrative issues associated with your tour.

Chapter 5 – Logistics

Thinking through your tour's logistical and administrative elements is not the most glamorous phase of this work, but it is critical to the tour's smooth operation and success.

Save the Date

When will the tour be offered? What date, day of the week and at what time? Can you tie it to a holiday or other event such as a festival? Is there an historical date that you can celebrate such as the town's founding, the birthdate of a famous citizen or the anniversary of a significant event in the neighborhood you'll be visiting?

Determine what other events will be occurring at the time you'd like to offer the tour. You'll be able to do most, if not all, of this research online. Check the community calendar of the local newspaper and school calendars. Visit the Chamber of Commerce's and the Visitors' Bureau's websites.

Don't forget to check the dates of sporting events such as the Super Bowl and World Series. Do you have a local sports team, even a college or high school team, lots of people follow? Their schedules are online.

Sometimes offering your tour during another event can work to your advantage. It depends on the nature of your program and your target audience. If you've designed something that will mainly appeal to women, Super Bowl Sunday might be the perfect time to run it. Although many women love football and would not want to miss the big game, there are plenty of others who'd jump at an interesting alternative to hours of TV sports.

Duration

How long should the tour last? People are busy and attention spans are growing shorter every day. The best length for a walking tour is 90 minutes. An hour is too short. People don't feel they've gotten their money's worth. Two hours is the outside edge. Anything over that is too long. If you have more than two hours of material, step back and fine-tune your focus. You either need to do some ruthless editing or you have more than one tour. That's a good thing!

Having said that, there are successful tours that run more than 90 minutes. For example, there is a popular offering in Santa Fe, New Mexico called Women of the West Historical Walking Tour that takes about three hours. The key is there is a coffee, snack and restroom break about half-way through the itinerary. If you are going past two hours you **must** provide a restroom stop.

How do you know how long your tour will really take? Rehearse it and time yourself. Walk the route at an appropriate pace. Do your full presentation at each stop. Then add some time.

You can never go faster than the slowest walker in your group. If you must cross streets, I promise you some of the participants will get stuck on the other side of the street until the light changes again. People will want to take pictures too. You don't want to force them to move along if they are really interested in something. They are the paying customers and you want them to enjoy themselves. I know these may seem like minor issues, but even a couple of these can add half an hour to your tour length. That's why aiming for 90 minutes is a good idea.

Frequency

How often do you plan to offer the tour? Is it a one-time special event? Will you offer it once a month? Every Saturday night? Just during October? You may not know for sure until you see how much interest the tour generates. Once you've done the hard work of putting the tour together, offering it multiple times becomes a simple routine. The more the guides work with the content and the route, the more comfortable they become and the more polished their performances become too.

Reservations and Ticketing

How do you plan to handle the customer check-in process? Will you require people to make reservations? If you are limiting the number of people who can participate, you probably should. Otherwise, you may have to turn people away at the tour site. That's not a good situation. Think carefully about whether you really need to limit participation. If you don't, the reservation requirement goes away.

If you feel you must limit attendance, who is going to handle reservations? How will that occur? By phone? In person? Online? What happens if people claim to have reservations and there's no record of them? What if you turn customers away because you think the program is full and people with reservations don't show up? You may not want to walk through that door. Don't overload tour operations with administrative tasks that don't contribute to the success of the program.

What about a minimum number of people? Will you operate the tour if just one person shows up? What if that person looks like a serial killer?

Will people need physical tickets? How will that work? Are you going to carry a roll of tickets around with you during the tour? Do you plan to take their money, give them a ticket and then take the ticket back? What if they lose their tickets?

The alternative is to allow people to simply walk up, pay and join the tour. No advance reservations, no sell-outs, no tickets. No administrative overhead.

If you are attracting huge crowds (good for you!) and feel you are losing control of who has and hasn't paid, get a sheet of cheap stickers, colorful little circles or stars or something like that, and have customers stick them to their shirts once they have paid. Your helper can be a real champion here.

There is one circumstance when you will need tickets: The open house tour. The host at each stop needs to determine whether people have paid. Tickets are an easy and obvious solution in this case. Set up ticketing at the first stop or in some central location. Maybe a merchant along the tour route would like you to set up in front of their shop.

Collect the money, give participants their tickets, a map of the tour route with addresses of the stops and explain how the program works. Make sure participants understand they need to show their ticket at each stop. You can buy a roll of cheap tickets at an office supply store or just print something. You could even combine the ticket, map, addresses and instructions into one document. If you print the material yourself, be sure to include your web address and an invitation to join your mailing list.

Costumes and Props

It is not necessary to wear a costume to guide a tour. When the guide is lively, fascinating and fun, it doesn't matter what he or she wears. A costume is an accessory. It's essentially a prop. The most fantastic costume in the world will not make a boring guide or a pointless tour interesting.

People have suggested that I wear a long black dress and carry a lantern when I guide my ghost tours. I'm a tee-shirt, shorts and tennis shoes sort of guide, but I understand where they're coming from. A costume would add atmosphere. But it would add a layer of complication to the operation too.

A long black dress might be fine in late October, but it would be unbearable on a sticky August night. What about slogging around in the rain? Having said all that, some people love to wear costumes. If that's you, by all means do so. Your audience will probably love it.

As far as the lantern goes, for me it's out of the question. It's an unnecessary distraction. I'd have to carry it through the entire tour. If it went out, I'd have to screw around with relighting it. It's a complication I don't want to deal with. But if you like the idea, try it and see how it goes.

Equipment

There are a few pieces of equipment you should consider. The first is a microphone and portable public address system. These are light, inexpensive and can make a huge difference to your customers.

Having a portable microphone can also help you attract guides. I know a couple of soft-spoken people who are wonderful presenters and love doing tours. There is no way they would or could raise their voices enough to be heard without a mic. It's a worthwhile investment.

Another useful gadget is a cheap laser pointer. It's great for drawing people's attention to interesting elements on buildings. If you're wandering around at night or going in old buildings, bring a flashlight. If you have a bag or backpack, toss in some extra lights for the participants. Don't forget spare batteries.

Visual Aids

Visual aids, such as old photographs or maps, enhance your tour and help participants imagine the way a building or street used to look. You can go low tech, print the images on plain paper and create a set of handouts. The trick is figuring out how many packets to prepare. Take your best guess and go with it. Be sure to add your web and email address to the handouts. Invite people to connect with you on social platforms and to subscribe to your email list to get updates about upcoming tours.

If you are doing an open house type tour where hosts are stationed at various stops and the participants travel from host to host, give the handouts and visual aides to the hosts. It's easier for stationary hosts to deal with paper handouts than it is for guides walking the tour route.

If you expect a small group, ten or less, you can load your material onto an iPad or other tablet and simply display the relevant images on the screen at the appropriate time.

Customer Questions

We will talk about marketing and promotion in Chapter 7. If you do a good job with that, people will get excited about the tour and they will have questions. How do you want them to contact you? By phone? On Facebook? Via email? Who is responsible for answering the questions? Again, if you work for an organization or company, this may be obvious.

Keep a list of the questions people ask. You can turn it into a Frequently Asked Questions (FAQ) page on your website. You can also make sure the top questions are addressed in future marketing materials.

These are the most common questions we get about Hidden Marietta's tours.

- Is there a bathroom break? Where? When? This is critical. It's not always possible to have a bathroom break on a tour. Let people know that is the case before they join the group. This is another reason to keep the tour length down to around 90 minutes.
- Is there anywhere to rest or sit down?
- I don't walk very well. Are there steps?
- How far do we go?
- I'm in a wheelchair. Can I go on the tour?
- Can we bring our five-year-old? How about our six-month-old? He's in a stroller and he's really quiet most of the time.
- Can we bring our dog? Believe it or not, this is the number one question we get. By the way, the answer is yes for Ghost Trek. Dogs cannot come on other tours, however.
- What about cameras? Can we take pictures? Videos? The answer to this should be a resounding yes! You want the tour participants to post their pictures on social media and tell everyone what fun they had. Word-of-mouth advertising is the best kind.
- Where should we park? Is it free? People won't attend if there's nowhere to park or it's too expensive. I realize this is outside your control, but it is an issue you need to address.

What about questions during the tour, questions about the stops or the material you're sharing? Let people know how you're going to handle this at the outset. It's not reasonable to expect them to hold their questions until the end of the tour. You could ask them, however, to wait until you finish your presentation at each stop and then open it up.

Follow the Rules

Do you need a guide's license? Do you have liability insurance? Should you? Do you need a permit to put a sandwich board or some other sort of sign out on the street? Do you need to collect and remit sales tax? Do you know which IRS rules and regulations apply to your situation?

Give yourself enough time to research these topics and to make sure you have cleared all the necessary hurdles. Ask your friendly local librarian to point you in the right direction or contact the Chamber of Commerce, Visitors' Bureau or small business section of your city or county government.

Chapter 6 - Money Matters

It's easy to over-complicate the financial side of things. This is where a lot of well-meaning people go off the rails. We aren't going to do that. We are going to stick to the basic financial issues surrounding your tour, including discussing how much you should charge.

Self-employed folks will have different issues than those developing tours as part of their duties at a salaried position. If you have questions regarding state, federal or local income taxes, FICA, allowable business deductions, retirement accounts, equipment depreciation, etc., consult a financial advisor, an accountant or your HR department.

Income vs Expenses

Every financial element related to your tour must fall into one of two categories. It is either income or it's an expense. Income minus expenses equals profit or loss. Income and profit are not synonymous.

For most of us the income side of the equation is fairly simple. It's the total amount we collect from the people who take the tour. It's the expense side where things get complicated. The most common expense error is missing something. This chapter will help you get your arms around all this.

Go through the following list and identify your costs. Make sure you have considered everything. Some items won't apply.

- Are you required to collect and remit state or local taxes of any sort such as sales taxes or user fees on the money you take in for the tour? At what rate?
- Do you need a license or permit? How much does it cost? Is this a one-time fee or a recurring expense?
- Sign and banners
- Flyers, posters, tickets, handouts, other printing expenses
- Advertising in newspapers, on isocial platforms or other media such as radio
- Website development, hosting costs, domain registrations, graphic designers
- Costumes and props
- Equipment such as flashlights, mics, batteries

- Office supplies such as paper, ink, tape, etc.
- Are paid staff working on the tour? Do you need to account for their compensation? Is anyone earning overtime? Do you have to reimburse anyone for mileage, parking or lunch?
- Do you have a guest expert such as a photographer or local celebrity coming along on the tour? Are you compensating that person? How much?
- Are you sharing profits or receipts with guides or other helpers? (See the discussion in Chapter 4 on Staffing)
- Are you making donations or paying commissions to venues or tour stops? (See the discussion below)
- Do you need insurance? How much does that cost?
- How much are your credit/debit card processing fees?
- Are you sharing receipts or income with any other organizations?
- Membership dues for the Visitors' Bureau, Main Street organization, etc.
- Other. All costs must be accounted for. If it doesn't fit anywhere else, list it here.

Add everything you identified to find the grand total.

If your total costs seem too high, go back through the list and determine which items can be deferred until you start making a profit. Look at each element and categorize it as mandatory, meaning you must spend the money now, or move it to a wish list.

Total the mandatory items only. Now we're ready for the next step.

How Much Should You Charge?

Look at your total mandatory costs, the items that cannot be deferred until later, then do some basic math. If your costs are $1000 and you plan to run the tour once, you either need to attract a huge crowd or charge a premium price. One hundred people at $10 each, 40 people at $25 or ten people at $100 will get you to breakeven. But how realistic are those scenarios?

This is where marketplace knowledge comes into play. How much do others charge for tours in your area? If you don't know, get online or get on the phone and find out.

If there are no tours in your town, look at neighboring towns. You need a benchmark. Keep looking until you find something comparable even if it's in a different state. If you discover the going rate for tours like the one you're planning is indeed $10, you need to think carefully about what you're doing.

A $10 tour can be extremely profitable, even with $1000 of costs, if you can run it often enough and attract enough customers. In this case, assuming you've identified all the costs and no new expenses pop up, you won't make money until customer number 101. How do you feel about that?

In the beginning, your costs really are the key factor. Be ruthless. Cut to the bare minimum.

The bottom line starts looking rosier much sooner with only $200 in costs to recover. That's breakeven at only 20 people paying $10. Let's say you run the tour every Saturday in July, four times, and 15 people show up each time. At the end of the month 60 people have participated. The total income is $600. With costs of $200 that yields a profit of $400. Now go to the wish list of deferred costs. You have a little extra cash to invest in a nice sign, get a logo designed or order some business cards.

Let's say the people who took the tour in July really liked it and told their friends. You're getting calls. People want to know when you're going to offer it again. You decide to do three more Saturdays in August and you raise the price to $15. You still get 15 people per weekend, but your income jumps to $675 even with one less tour session. You kept costs down by making your own flyers and buying some super cheap posters for $25. Profit this time around is $650.

The best and most realistic way to look at this example is as a single two-month tour season. Total income was $1275. Total costs were $225. Total profit is $1050. Now we're talking.

Discounts

Decide whether you will offer child and/or senior discounts. I guarantee you'll be asked for both. Think it through and make a conscious choice. Having participants who are paying less than full price in the customer mix means you need to attract more people to reach the breakeven point.

Group discounts are a different sort of issue. We will discuss that in Chapter 7 on Marketing and Promotion.

Let's work through a couple more examples.

If your total mandatory costs are $750 and the tour rate is $15, you need 50 customers to break even. If you are offering kids or seniors discounts, or incurring debit/credit card fees, however, you'll need to attract more people. Let's say you are charging $15 for adults and $10 for kids and seniors. 50 people turn out for the tour but 15 of them qualify for the lower price. You took in $675. You missed breaking even by $75.

If you are going to be paying guides, venues or other organizations based on receipts or turnout, you need to add that factor to the equation too. Let's say you are going to be paying out 25% of receipts off the top. For the sake of simplicity, let's say everyone who turns out is a full-paying adult.

You lucked out! 60 people showed up at $15 each. Total receipts are $900. You owe 25% or $225 to the guide. You cleared $675. You're still in the hole for $75!

You need to run the tour again, raise your price or cut your costs **if you want to make money**. Not everyone does. As we said at the outset, there are many reasons to offer tours. Even if you are running the tour for non-monetary reasons, it's good to know whether it is profitable or not.

You don't need to become a penny-pinching miser and you don't want your promotional material to look cheesy. But keeping costs as low as you reasonably can is the best way to increase your chance of long-term success.

Donations and Commissions

It's wonderful when businesses and building owners let you bring your group into their premises for free. It doesn't always work that way though.

There are a couple of ways to compensate venues for giving you access for the tour. The first and simplest way is to offer a flat fee. If you've never done the tour before, it's hard to know what that amount should be. Tour frequency is a factor too. If this is a brand-new tour and it's only going to be offered once, you just have to take your best shot. If you offer $75 and only five people show up at $10 per person, you're in the hole for $25. On the other hand, if 50 people show up, $75 might seem just about right.

If the tour is going to be offered several times or is ongoing, you have other options. You could start with a flat fee and as you get attendance information, transition to a portion of receipts. Ten percent, a dollar per person, 50 cents per person, it will depend on how much you're charging and how critical the stop is to the tour's success. If your tour falls apart without the stop, make sure you're sharing enough to keep the venue happy and the welcome mat out.

Multiple Organizations

If you are collaborating with another organization or tour operator and you are going to split the profit, make sure you spell out how this is going to be computed in advance and **get it in writing**. Again, income does not equal profit.

Let's say you are working with a local historical preservation group. They have agreed to promote the tour to their members for 25% of the receipts. You are charging $10 per person and 20 people show up. Your income is $200. You owe the preservation group 25% or $50. Any costs you incurred for the tour must be covered out of your remaining $150. If you had $75 in printing costs, a newspaper ad and flashlight batteries, your final profit on the tour is $75.

If your agreement with the historical preservation group was for 25% of the profit (as opposed to the receipts or income), then the first thing you do is subtract your $75 cost from the $200 income which leaves a profit of $125. Now you owe the preservation group 25% of $125 or $31.25. Your final profit on the tour is $93.75.

There's something to be said for the simple approach of just giving 25% off the top and it's perfectly fine to agree to that sort of arrangement. Just understand what you're agreeing to. Know your costs and do the math first.

Specify in writing who is responsible for what and how payment amounts will be determined. This doesn't have to be super complicated. It just has to be clear.

This is a basic agreement we used for an open house style event.

Sample Collaboration Agreement

Responsibilities:

Party A –

- Identify and secure access to five downtown buildings to serve as venues
- Cover all paid promotion and advertising expenses
- Arrange for and cover the cost of all printing and materials, posters, programs, tickets, etc.
- Arrange volunteers to staff venues not covered by HM and to work at the reception table, sell tickets and collect money
- Provide liability insurance to all venues and HM

HM –

- Research and write blurbs and background information/stories on venues
- Provide digital images when available
- Provide volunteers for two venues

- Promote the event on the HM Facebook page, website and newsletter

Ticket Price and Revenue Sharing:

- Tickets will be $15. No discounts. $10 goes to Party A and $5 goes to HM.

Cash or Credit

Will you accept credit/debit cards? If you work for a company or organization, all the systems you need for payments and processing may already be in place. Check with the powers-that-be. If you're operating independently, you'll need to make some decisions.

You can become a credit/debit card vendor. But there is a fee for each transaction and there may be other fees as well. You either need to increase your tour price to cover those new costs or accept the fact that you will be receiving less than the full amount for a portion of your audience.

Accepting credit/debit cards also opens you to charge backs or refund requests from the credit card companies. This may be OK. Offering this convenience to your customers may outweigh the complications. Like other matters in the financial arena, go in with your eyes open.

Even if you work for an organization that is a credit/debit card vendor, things can get complicated. How are you going to physically process the cards? It's getting easier all the time to run transactions through smart phones. However, if you are offering the tour away from your home office, you'll need to determine whether you can accept cards at a remote location on behalf of your organization.

Hidden Marietta does not accept checks or credit/debit cards for public tours. We make it clear in our promotional materials that cash is required. So far this has not been a problem, although it's something we will have to revisit one of these days.

I realize many people don't carry much money. I'm one of them. I love my debit and credit cards. But as a businessperson I'm not willing to pay processing fees on a $15 tour. I also don't want to swipe cards and get signatures on the street. You may make a different choice.

Even if you accept credit/debit cards, make sure to have plenty of change in the correct denominations on hand for those who do pay with cash. For example, if your tour costs $15, you'll need lots of five-dollar bills because almost everyone is going to hand you a $20. If the tour costs $7, make sure you have lots of one-dollar bills. Think it through.

The best advice on checks is don't accept them. Make an exception for groups from companies or organizations you have been working with and know.

Getting paid should be the easy part, but there are a few potential pitfalls to be aware of. **Collect the money before the tour begins**. You can make exceptions for groups who have made payment arrangements in advance.

Unfortunately, occasionally, a group will try to dodge out on their payment obligation. Here is a sample Payment Demand Letter. Feel free to copy and adapt it to your heart's content. Send it through the mail, certified, return receipt requested. I hope you don't need it.

Sample Payment Demand Letter

Sirs:

On or about (Date), (Name of the person who made the booking), (Job title), a representative of your company made arrangements for my company, Hidden Marietta, LLC, to perform services in the manner of a tour for (number) employees of your company.

Upon promise to pay Two Hundred Ten dollars ($210 or whatever it was) by Mr. (or Ms.) X, such services were performed on (Date). Confirming emails are attached.

I have billed your company for services performed, have received confirmation from Mr. (or Ms.) X that he (she) would ensure such payment would be made. Subsequently, I have received no payment, no return emails, no return phone calls, or any other such correspondence as would indicate your company is adhering to its obligation to pay for services performed.

I can only conclude that your accounts payable department is unaware of this just debt and must therefore bring it to your attention.

Please consider this letter with attachments a demand for payment in full.

Sincerely,

Refunds

If you don't require or accept payments in advance, you don't have to deal with no shows. You also dramatically reduce the number of refund requests. Nevertheless, refund situations still arise.

- Unhappy customers – Some people hate everything and they are going to hate your tour too. If you are unfortunate enough to have one of these folks in your tour group and they start complaining and want their money back, give it to them. Don't argue. Focus on the rest of the group and move on.
- Unruly customers – Some people are so loud, disruptive and/or offensive, you want them to leave the tour. Give them their money back and move on.
- Tour disruption/interruption – What do you do when you're half-way through your tour and the heavens open? This has happened to me more than once. Even though I feel I've earned my pay since the tour is half over, I look at the people, soaking wet, bedraggled, not having anything close to a good time and I offer to give their money back. Most of them take me up on it. It's tough to pull a big wad of cash out of your pocket and return it, but it's the right way to handle it. There are usually a few hardy souls who continue to the bitter end. Many of those who go home early come back at a later time. You can bet they tell everyone about how well they were treated. Goodwill and positive word of mouth are worth much more than one evening's tour receipts, even when it happens on your biggest night.

Effective marketing and promotion are the keys to getting customers to turn out in the first place. That's where we're heading next.

Chapter 7 – Marketing and Promotion

Effective marketing and promotion are critical to your tour's success. Look at the big picture and plan your campaign as early as you can, at least two months in advance if you can swing it.

Before you embark on the promotional and marketing phase of tour development, you need to answer one very important question: Who is your target audience?

If you don't know who your ideal customers are, you won't know how best to reach them. You won't know where to concentrate your marketing efforts. A tour aimed at millennial ghost hunters needs to be promoted differently than one designed to appeal to the members of the senior center's genealogy club.

If your target audience listens to the radio and you put an ad in the newspaper, you've not only wasted money, you've missed an opportunity to connect. The same thing applies to social platforms. Posting endless Twitter updates about the tour will be pointless if your audience spends all their time on Facebook.

As you consider your promotional options, and there are many, remember this is not an all or nothing proposition. Take an integrated approach and use as many channels and platforms as you can comfortably manage.

Defining Your Audience

So, who is your target audience? Anyone with $20 is not an acceptable response. Ask yourself a few basic questions. If everything goes just as planned and the perfect people show up for your tour, who will they be?

A lot of this is admittedly guesswork. But taking a stab at the answers will help you design a more effective marketing campaign. It will help you design a better tour too.

- How old are your ideal customers? 65? 23? 9?
- Are they mostly men or women?
- What are they interested in? We assume local history, but what aspects? Architecture? Businesses of the past? Any particular time period? Is this more of a nostalgia or a history crowd?
- What else are they interested in? Food? Beer? Art? Flowers? Vintage cars? Can you work any of those elements into the tour experience?

- How much do they already know about the tour's topic?
- Are they local people or tourists from somewhere else? Where?
- Do they or did they live in the neighborhood?
- Do you know them or will they be complete strangers?

Now that you have an idea of the type of person you'd like to reach, go a little further. How does this person get information about local events? The paper? Facebook? Radio? By seeing a poster in a downtown shop window? Ask around. Talk to people. Accept the fact that you're probably going to have to make some assumptions and educated guesses too.

Cost Factors

You can spend a lot of money very quickly on ads and other promotional pieces and activities. There are plenty of people who will tell you that paid marketing is the only way to make your tour succeed. Those people are wrong.

A much better plan, especially in the beginning, is to start where you are with what you know and what you have. You can adjust, adapt and upgrade as you go along.

This means saying no to spending big bucks on ads and opting instead for self-produced flyers and posters. It means passing on paid social media promotions and using free social sharing instead. As your tour or tours grow and you learn more about who is actually showing up, who your real customers are in other words, fine-tune your efforts. As the target becomes clearer, it's easier to hit.

The most important question is not how much does it cost? The most important question is where do my customers consume information and how can I reach them? For a few very specific target markets the answer will be obvious. Everyone belongs to the same organization and they have a newsletter. Or there are hundreds of active, engaged people in a Facebook group dedicated to discussing the neighborhood you're going to tour. It's usually not that easy though. The answer is almost always a combination of various types of outreach. Let's look at the possibilities.

You probably won't use all the following outlets or platforms. Record the details in your notebook or folder for those that you do plan to use.

Traditional Media

Traditional media includes newspapers, magazines, direct mail, print newsletters, radio, television, posters, billboards, rack cards and brochures. Traditional media exposure is usually something you pay for, but it can be free. You might be invited to talk about your upcoming tour on a local radio show, for example. If you work for a nonprofit or a community group is sponsoring or will benefit from the tour, media outlets may give you some coverage as a public service.

The smaller your media market, the more likely it is you'll get free exposure. If you live in a major metropolitan area, the odds of getting your tour covered on TV or in the paper are slim. However, most media outlets are more lenient about the kind of material that appears online. Make sure you're checking all the angles. And don't forget weekly neighborhood newspapers or free local entertainment guides. They are often looking for material.

Many traditional media outlets have surprisingly long lead times. Get online or call them and find out how it works in your town. You will probably need to submit the information about your tour via a press release or by filling out an online form.

Press releases often end up in the trash because a lot of them look like spam. Make sure yours gets read. Here's a simple, straightforward example.

Sample Press Release

New Historic Cambridge Tour

From: Dickens Victorian Village

Event: Harvest Home Tour

Date: October 3, 2014

Time: 5:00pm – 7:00pm

Location: Red Brick District, Downtown Cambridge

Description:

Experience the beauty and historic charm of downtown Cambridge as Dickens Victorian Village and the Guernsey County Historical Museum present the first Harvest Home Tour.

Help us inaugurate the Red Brick District historic neighborhood, the original residential quarter near the courthouse. Enjoy exclusive access to the interiors of six homes representing a variety of time periods and architectural styles. Hear the stories of these magnificent houses and the people who lived there.

Guests will be greeted by a costumed host/hostess at each residence. Fall refreshments will be served on the front porches.

Tickets are $10. Purchase tickets and begin the tour at the Dickens Welcome Center, 745 Steubenville Avenue.

Contact: Lynne Sturtevant, phone, email address

Don't over-complicate things. Posters and flyers can be surprisingly effective and they work whether you're offering the tour once or on an ongoing basis. This is where having a catchy title really helps. A good image, either a drawing, a photograph you took yourself or a vintage one you know is copyright free, is all you need.

If you don't know how to create an attractive flyer, ask your friends or kids to help. There are also free websites that allow even the most design-challenged beginners to create professional-looking flyers, handouts and other items. My favorite is Canva which is at canva.com.

Don't lose sleep over this. Just do your best. Get some colored paper and go for it. Make sure the flyer includes the following elements:

- Name of tour
- Where
- When – date, day of week and time
- How much
- Tell people how to sign up or tell them reservations are **not** required
- How do they get more information – phone and web address
- Who is sponsoring this or putting it on

Once you have the flyers, take them around town. Ask permission to place them in shops, restaurants, bars and other businesses that have lots of foot traffic. Use the opportunity to tell everyone about your tour, answer questions and invite people to attend. Start building buzz!

Do businesses in your target neighborhood put posters for upcoming events in their windows? Contact a print shop and find out how much it would cost to get a few made.

Think about getting a sign. We use a vinyl sandwich board. One side advertises Ghost Trek, a tour that runs twice a week for five months. The other side is a chalk board we can use for one-time tours or anything we like. This has turned out to be a very useful piece of equipment and was not too expensive. We put it out early in the morning on tour days and pick it up at the end of each evening. Since it's temporary, we don't need a permit or any other kind of clearance to use it. Check with the powers-that-be regarding signage in your jurisdiction before you follow this route.

New Media

New media, also known as digital media, includes websites, blogs, Facebook, Twitter, YouTube, Pinterest, Instagram, LinkedIn and other social platforms as well as email newsletters.

Using digital media to promote your tour can be easy, effective and dirt cheap. But you must follow the rules of online etiquette. Do not spam. People may be happy to allow you to promote your tour on their sites or pages, but you **must** get permission first. I remove unauthorized posts and links from my sites the minute I spot them. If it happens twice, I block the offending person or account forever. End of story.

Your Website

As soon as you have the details of your tour nailed down, add a page to your website, a page devoted exclusively to the new tour. Use color, different size fonts and images. Make it attractive! Make it interesting! Be sure to include all the information your potential customers need. Encourage them to ask questions via your comment system and/or contact form. Include a telephone number too.

As you start to design your new page, select a dramatic image to use as the thumbnail. Google and other services like Yahoo and Bing will pull the thumbnail picture into their search results. Help potential customers find the tour page by writing a short, clear and appealing description, approximately 100 characters. Either add it to the SEO (search engine optimization) section in your site's administrative dashboard or use it as the lead sentence or sentences on the page.

Every time you post something about the tour on social platforms or on other websites, include a link back to the tour page, not to your home page.

If you have a blog, write a post about the tour. Talk about why you chose the route, what you think people will get from the experience. Go into detail about some of the stops. Raise some intriguing questions. Ask readers what they know about this part of town. Ask them to tell you what other types of tours or areas they'd like to explore in the comments.

When tour season ends or your one-time event is over, don't delete the tour page. Hide or unpublish it. When the time comes to promote the tour again, update the information, add a new photo or two, hit publish and boom! You're back in business. Even if you never offer that specific tour again, you can use the page as a template for other programs.

Coordinating with Other Organizations

If you are collaborating with another organization such as a Main Street or neighborhood group, make sure they link to the tour page on your website. Encourage them to add a page promoting the tour to their site as well.

Be sure to include the names, logos and links for all partner organizations and any official sponsors on your tour page.

There may be other organizations or groups that would allow you to place tour information and a link on their sites. Are you a member of the Visitors' Bureau? Chamber of Commerce? How about the historical society? Are any businesses stops on the tour?

Even if the other organization doesn't have a website or email list, they may allow you to mail a flyer to their members or let you display tour information in their office. It doesn't hurt to ask.

Email Newsletters

If you have a newsletter – and you should! – announce the upcoming tour to your list. You don't have to tell them everything in the newsletter. Use the short description you wrote for SEO purposes, add an interesting photo – not the same one that's on your site – and a link back to the tour page for full information. Add social share buttons and encourage your subscribers to share the information with anyone they think might be interested.

You will probably get new visitors to your site this way so make sure you have an email list sign-up box on the tour page. Invite people to subscribe by saying something like, "Join us and be the first to know about other great tours focusing on downtown Evanston."

Social Platforms and Networks

Facebook, Twitter, Pinterest, Instagram and YouTube are built for sharing information, pictures, videos and links. You don't have to be on all of them. You just have to be where your customers and the people you want to become your customers are.

If you're not sure what platforms your audience uses, ask them. Ask people who come to your attraction, those who wait on you in restaurants, store clerks, people in line at the bank. This isn't a scientific sampling; it's informal information gathering. And don't make the mistake of assuming older people are not using social media. They are.

It's beyond the scope of this book to delve into the mechanics of posting on the various platforms, but a few general guidelines will help your posts reach more potential customers.

- I said this before, but it bears repeating. Don't spam people, groups or business pages. If you want to post information about your tour on someone else's page or site, ask permission *first*.
- Use pictures and/or video.
- Don't try to cram all the tour details into a post or tweet. It will be too long and no one will read it. Say enough to raise interest then provide a link back to the tour page on your website.
- Create an Event in Facebook.
- Ask people to share your content and thank them when they do.
- Respond to any questions or comments as soon as you can.
- Post several times, at different times of day. Social media feeds move very quickly. Not everyone sees every post. You can use the same text but change the picture each time you post.
- After the event, send a post or tweet thanking people for coming. Include a picture of the actual tour if you can.

Speaking

Public speaking is an easy and effective way to promote your tour. It doesn't have to be an elaborate presentation in front of a huge crowd. There are many small groups that meet on a regular basis, some as often as weekly. Think Lions, Rotary and other community and service clubs. There are garden clubs, alumni organizations and church groups. You can probably find out who meets when by checking the community calendar in the newspaper. The folks who put programs together for meetings are always looking for speakers. The presentations are usually short, 20 - 30 minutes, and the audiences are friendly and attentive. Sometimes you even get lunch!

Pull out a few interesting tidbits you discovered in your research, share background information on the neighborhood or area you're going to be visiting or talk about the time period you'll be focusing on. Don't forget your flyers.

Attracting Groups

Groups are a great addition to your customer base. There are several advantages to working with them. They are predictable. They book in advance. You know how many people are coming and when. Plus, they can represent a significant new income stream.

There are many types of groups. Groups formed by tour operators are potential customers. These folks usually arrive on buses. The best way to find groups of this sort is through your Visitors' Bureau. Group tour operators need new angles and are always looking for interesting new components to add to their programs. Your tour may fit nicely into a larger itinerary.

Don't forget about local groups. There are plenty of clubs that might enjoy taking your tour as a private group activity: antique clubs, service clubs, reading groups, scout troops and even people organizing big family reunions.

Local history can reinforce a community's sense of identity and be a source of pride in the town's story. Think about corporate groups interested in heritage, community development and historic preservation as well as libraries, museums, real estate agent associations and merchant/retail groups.

Can you tweak your tour to make it more appealing to specific groups? Could you add something about when the big trees that line the streets were planted for the garden club?

Sometimes tweaking means subtracting material. Ghost Trek is not designed for kids. Some of the stories are complicated and nuanced plus there are references to prostitution and embalming. I created a G-rated version of the tour that is only an hour long and operates in the afternoon. The tour has been the featured activity for several birthday parties.

Groups expect and should receive a discount. Develop a price chart based on the group size so you don't have to figure out the rate every time the question comes up. Here's an example for a tour that normally costs $20.

- 1-9 people - $20 per person
- 10-19 people - $15 per person
- 20-29 people - $10 per person
- 30+ people - $7 per person

Freebies

You will probably be asked for free tour passes at some point. Whether or not you agree depends on who they are for and how often your tour runs.

I always offer free passes to people who work for the Visitors' Bureau, local hotel staff, members of the media including travel bloggers and group leaders or organizers. This is Marketing 101.

I get quite a few requests from nonprofits for passes that they can raffle or use as prizes. I always say yes. The passes are for a tour that does not have a limit on the number of participants. The complimentary folks are not displacing paying customers in other words. The tour is running anyway and I'm glad to have them along. This creates a lot of goodwill in the community.

I developed the following simple one-page gift certificate for this purpose. Feel free to adapt it to your programs.

Sample Gift Certificate

Congratulations!

You and a guest are invited to a complimentary Ghost Trek walking tour of historic and haunted downtown Marietta!

Ghost Trek departs from the fountain across from the Lafayette Hotel at the corner of Front and Greene Streets every Friday and Saturday evening at 8pm, weather permitting. Reservations are not required.

The 2014 season of Ghost Trek starts on Friday, June 6 and ends on Saturday, November 1, 2014.

Ghost Trek lasts about an hour and a half. Wear comfortable walking shoes and bring your camera. You never know what we might encounter!

This certificate does not apply to private tours. Valid only on public Ghost Treks. Ghost Trek does not operate Sternwheel Festival weekend, September 5 and 6, 2014. Not valid after November 1, 2014. No cash value and no refund for unused portions. For more information call 740-629-1805 or go to www.hiddenmarietta.com

Please give this certificate to the tour guide to claim your free Ghost Trek. Thank you!

If you plan to limit attendance and the tour is likely to sell out or if you are only running the tour once or twice, I'm not sure what advantage you would gain by offering free passes. But that is something you will have to decide based on your situation.

If you are collaborating with others, find out if they expect free passes for anyone, board members, staff, etc. It's best to know in advance.

Vintage Images

We discussed how and where to find vintage photos and other images in Chapter 2 on Research. We also covered issues relating to copyrights. Refer to that section if you have questions or concerns.

Adding vintage images to your tour's promotional material is a great idea. If you're short on photos, put out a call for images on social media. Tell people about the tour and see what turns up. You could frame the request as a contest. Give the person who submits the best image a free pass.

Images that show the neighborhood or specific buildings at various times work best. Advertisements from the companies or shops that used to be there, even old postcards can be used to promote the tour.

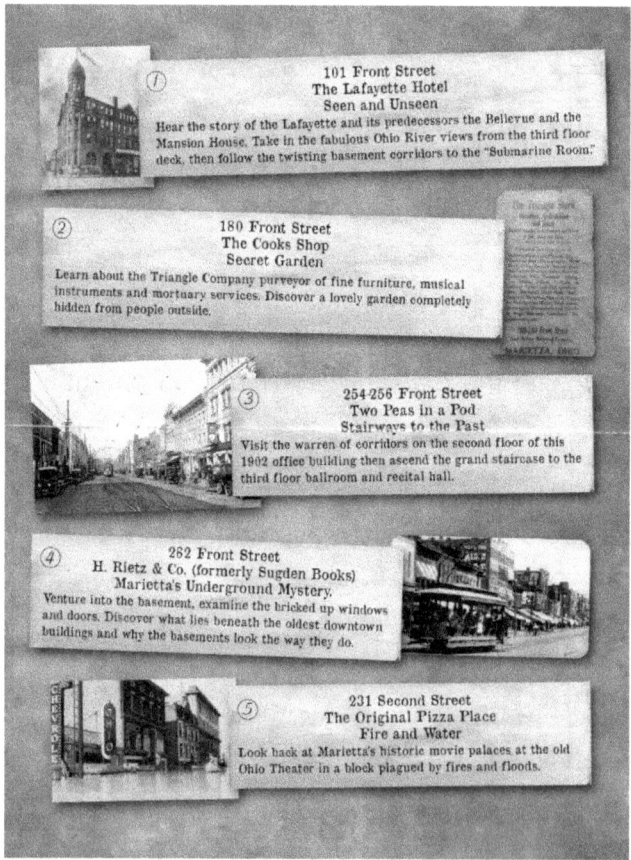

You can also create a nice handout with vintage images you can give to tour participants as a souvenir. Make sure you include your contact information and an invitation to join your email list, visit your Facebook page, donate to the historical society or whatever action you'd like people to take.

Your marketing efforts are starting to pay off. You're building buzz. Tour day is just around the corner and lots of people have told you they plan to attend. You're feeling great! And why shouldn't you?

What could possibly go wrong?

Chapter 8 – Tour Day: What Could Possibly Go Wrong?

It's show time! The big day has finally arrived. All your hard work is about to pay off. Or is it?

A Cautionary Tale

Ghost Trek was so successful its first year, I decided to add a second tour the following summer. Several enormous ancient Indian mounds dot the historic neighborhood adjacent to downtown Marietta. Not only were there no regularly scheduled tours of the mounds, there was almost no information available to tourists or local folks interested in exploring these structures. So, I created the Ancient Earthworks Tour.

I wanted to keep things as simple as possible, so I decided not to require reservations. I had flyers and rack cards printed that said the tour operated every Saturday and Sunday at 2pm and told people to meet in Mound Cemetery where the largest and most spectacular earthwork is located. I put the flyers and cards all over town.

The first day for the tour was Saturday, June 6. Three people showed up. OK, I thought, we're off to a slow start, but it will build over time. The next day no one came for the tour. In fact, no additional customers appeared until Saturday, July 4 – a whole month later – when two adults and a child took the tour.

I had two problems. The first was I didn't know why people were not coming to Ancient Earthworks. Was it because they didn't know about the tour? Were they not interested? Or was something else going on? My second problem related to the promotional material I had spread all over town. It stated that reservations were not required. I did not want someone to show up for the tour and find no one there to meet them. That meant I had to go to the cemetery every Saturday and Sunday at 2pm that entire summer.

Things never really picked up. By the end of August, a grand total of 21 people had gone on the Ancient Earthworks Tour. I figured I could change things up at that point, so I raised the price from $10 to $15 and made it a private, reservations required experience. I still offer the tour to groups of six or more. It's an interesting tour and the people who take it really like it. But it never caught on. I'm still not sure why.

There are so many ways tours can go awry. Some issues are huge; some are minor. Every one of them is annoying. It's impossible to control every situation or plan for every contingency. Trying to do so would be a colossal waste of energy. However, it's worthwhile to spend some time thinking about how you will handle various situations. Then if they do arise, you won't be immobilized because you'll have already figured out Plan B.

Weather Woes

You can't control the weather, but you can work around it to some extent. It's just part of the game when you offer outdoor tours. The Ghost Trek tour operates every Friday and Saturday night from the first weekend in June through the last weekend in October. Sometimes it rains. Generally, we go anyway. The guide brings an umbrella. It's not that big of a deal. We get a much smaller crowd than normal, of course, but a few people always show up, usually out-of-town visitors who cannot come back on a drier night.

As incredible as it sounds, we have only had to cancel the tour due to weather twice in seven years, both times because of severe thunderstorms.

Our policy on weather cancelations is the guide on duty makes the call. Because we don't take reservations in advance, we don't know how many people are planning to attend and we don't have a way to contact them individually. The guide goes to the tour starting point at the regular time and assesses the situation. If she decides to cancel, she stays until about ten minutes after the tour is scheduled to start so that she can explain what's happening to customers on site.

Storms aren't the only weather condition that can cause problems. Walking around outside in the bitter cold can be utterly miserable and slippery sidewalks are dangerous. The heat isn't much better. I've had seniors on swelteringly hot, humid days that looked really bad by the end of the tour. Keep your eye on your customers. If you need to suspend the tour in the middle of the route and give everyone a refund, do it. Be a rational, responsible adult.

If your tour runs regularly and you need to cancel, it's not that big of a deal. If the tour is a one-time event, however, you'll need to make some decisions. Will you reschedule? When? How will you let people know? The answers to these questions will vary depending on whether you take reservations.

People You Depend On

Sometimes the people you're depending on, the ones who promised to help you, bail out at the last minute or simply don't show up. If it's almost tour time, the reasons they don't appear are irrelevant. There will be plenty of time to hash that over later, if you're so inclined. Right now, you've got a tour to run. If there's no guide, you must step in. You do have a copy of the tour script with you, don't you? You know, the one you stuck in your backpack so you'd be prepared if the guide forgot his?

If you're the guide and your helper is a no-show, you're on your own. It's great to have a helper along with you, but you can certainly run the tour without one. If someone else is serving as the guide and they are uncomfortable without a helper, guess what? You're up. This might be a blessing in disguise. You can unobtrusively observe your guide. You can also get a feel for how the tour participants like the program. What parts bore them? What parts deserve more time?

If you've invited an expert along, a professional photographer to give the group picture-taking tips or an architectural historian to point out the finer features of certain buildings, and that person doesn't show, you've got a decision to make. If the expert was the main draw for the tour, you might have to cancel. But before you do, ask yourself if there's any way to salvage the program. Be honest. Tell people what has happened. They have traveled to the site to participate. They may want to come along anyway. Do you have enough material to offer the tour on your own? Could you give them a discount? Believe it or not, these things sometimes turn out to be more fun than they would have been if the expert had been along.

Touching Base

Contact everyone who js supposed to work on the tour – guides, helpers, experts, people who are opening venues and anyone else involved – two days before the event and verify they are onboard. If you possibly can, talk to these people either in person or by phone. If that's not an option, email, send a text, Facebook message them, whatever you have to do. **Make sure you get a response.**

Self-Inflicted Wounds

What if you're the one who causes the problem?

You're the guide. You don't have a backup or a helper because you are a one-person operation. You've poured your heart and soul into this. You wake up on tour day with the worst case of laryngitis in recorded history. Or your voice is fine, but you trip over your cat and sprain your ankle. Or as the day goes on you realize there is no way you can be more than three or four feet from a bathroom. You're OK but a family member becomes ill or has an emergency of some sort.

What are you going to do? I don't have the answer. You probably don't either, but this is something you need to think through. Decide how you are going to handle this sort of situation before it arises.

I did tours alone for five years. I was never sick on a tour day, although I did step in a hole one time and twist my ankle. By the time the tour started, I was good to go. But that was pure luck.

Traffic Jams

Arriving late for your own tour is ridiculous. There is absolutely no excuse for this. Here's how to make sure it doesn't happen: Plan ahead!

Arrive at the tour departure point at least half an hour before the tour is scheduled to start. If people join the tour by simply walking up and paying, get there 45 minutes early. You may end up standing around killing time. That's good. That means your potential customers will find a person waiting for them when they arrive. No one will show up and wonder what they're supposed to do, who they're supposed to talk to, etc.

If you must drive to the tour location, do a practice run and time it. Do it on the same day of the week, at the same time you will really be traveling. In other words, if the tour is going to be on Saturday at 2pm, don't do a practice run on Tuesday morning.

Once you know how long it takes, double your travel time. The same rule applies if you're walking, taking a taxi or bus, whatever.

If you are driving, figure out where you are going to park. Identify a couple of alternatives in case you encounter full lots, road closures, detours, etc. Make sure you have enough gas.

Does this sound like overkill? It's a lot better than sitting in traffic or frantically circling the neighborhood looking for a parking place as you watch the minutes tick down to your scheduled departure time.

Lock Outs

What if you're going inside one historic building? It's the main attraction, the thing everyone wants to see, the thing the whole tour is built around. When you arrive with your group right on schedule, the door is locked, the lights are off. Not a living soul in sight. Variations on this theme include keys that don't work, security alarms that go off and neighbors who call the police. Make sure you and the building owner know exactly how this stop is going to work. Who is responsible for opening the venue? When will that happen? Who is responsible for closing? Who do you contact if you have a problem and how? Practice it. Go there – in the dark if your tour will be at night – and try the key. Make sure you know what you're doing in advance.

Check Then Double Check

No matter how well you plan, things go wrong. The best approach is to check and double check equipment, routes, venues, etc. Then do your best.

Payment Processing

If people will be paying in cash, make sure to bring enough change. In our promotional pieces we remind folks our tours are cash only and that exact change is greatly appreciated. Nevertheless, every couple of weeks someone shows up with a $100 bill.

If you are accepting credit/debit cards, make sure you have your processing device with you and that it is working.

Handouts

If you have handouts, make them in advance. Don't wait until the day of the tour or even the day before. Leave enough time to finish preparing the handouts even if the printer breaks, you run out of paper, or there is a massive power failure. Just do what you need to in order to get your collateral material ready ahead of time. Period.

Equipment Failures

You arrive at the dark and creepy abandoned theater, the high point of your tour, you reach into the box of flashlights you have cleverly stashed in the lobby and none of them work. The batteries are dead. If you had stopped at the theater that afternoon or the day before and checked, you would have had time to get new batteries. This stuff is obvious. This stuff is easy. Think ahead.

Your microphone doesn't work. Again, check the battery the day before or as early as you can. If you can charge it or get it fixed, do it. If not, go without. This goes for all electronics and battery-powered devices.

Detours

You arrive at the tour departure point and the sidewalks along your intended route are closed. There are city trucks and workers all over the place and they're pouring concrete. This type of disruption happens more often than you might guess. The best precautionary measure is to be aware of what's going on in the neighborhood and along the tour route. However, some things are not predictable. You will have to decide whether you can still run the tour. Sometimes you must reschedule. Other times you can figure out a way to work around the obstacle.

Each year there is one fall evening when Ghost Trek is disrupted by a huge street party. My preferred approach would be to reroute the tour and avoid the party entirely. However, it takes place at our final stop, the coolest and most surprising on the tour. At our next-to-last stop we tell our folks what to expect. "We are coming up on our last stop. There's a big football party going on down there with a lot of happy people, a lot of beer and a lot of noise. So, let's talk about what we are going to see now while we can do it without yelling."

We also occasionally encounter problems in a hotel lobby that is a regular stop on one of our tours. We usually sit in the lobby and talk about the building and its history for about 15 minutes. It can be very pleasant and is a rest break for our older customers. However, it can also be noisy, crowded and chaotic, depending on what's going on around town, if groups are in, etc. Other times there are wedding parties and the lobby has been completely rearranged. The best plan is to stop in and check things out before the tour. If it looks like a stop is going to be a problem, plan to cut it short, or eliminate it completely. It's good to have an extra stop or a few extra stories in your repertoire that you can fall back on to fill the time if you need them.

Timing

A common problem, especially on a new tour, is timing, the tour's length. It's either too short or too long. This improves with practice. Keep an eye on your watch. If you are running fast, the tour is not long enough, slow down. Walk slower. Talk slower. Point out more things. Ask people if they have questions. Ask them what they know about the neighborhood. If it's not a delivery problem and you really don't have enough material, you need to fix that before the next tour.

The other extreme is that you're running too long. This is easy to fix. Stop talking. Move to the next stop. Cut things out if you have to. If you've told people the tour will last 90 minutes, they aren't going to think they are getting something extra if you draw things out for two hours.

Sometimes it's not you but the participants that make the tour run long. They are lollygagging around, taking pictures, etc. That's fine. It probably means they're having a good time. But you need to stay on schedule. Say something like, "We have more interesting things to see so let's move on."

You also must accommodate slow walkers. The group can only go as fast as the slowest person. You must adjust, slow down and set an appropriate pace. I'm a fast walker and this is harder than it sounds. Cut a stop if you need to.

Duh . . .

Everyone's worst fear is that they'll go blank and completely forget their material. I'm sorry to tell you this, but that will happen at some point. Fortunately, it's easy to deal with. Have your script in your pocket. Pull it out and say something like, "I want to make sure I get this right." People don't care if you look at notes. They are on the tour because they are interested in the topic or the neighborhood. They want the information.

In fact, in the beginning, it's a great idea to have your script along. You'll feel more confident and you'll do a better job. You'll be surprised how fast you memorize the material, especially for tours you're running frequently.

Human Obstacles and Competition

The most preposterous obstacle I've encountered so far arrived in the form of two very officious men who were coordinating events for a weekend of boat races on the Ohio River. I place my sandwich board sign next to a large public fountain on the riverbank. That's our meeting point and where the tour begins. I put it out every Friday morning, take it home at the end of Friday's tour, put it back out on Saturday morning and take it home at the end of that evening. The whole process repeats every weekend for five months.

When I arrived at the fountain on this Friday morning to put up my sign, the boat racing officials informed me that I needed to pay them to have my sign at the fountain. They gave me a choice. I could either become a vendor or an official sponsor of their event. They wanted several hundred dollars.

I told them the fountain was my place of business, that I was there every weekend and that, unlike them, I ran an ongoing operation at this location. I also told them if they didn't back off, I would take the matter up with the mayor's office. I had no idea whether the city would do anything. I was basically bluffing, but they backed down.

If your tour is ongoing and you begin attracting decent sized groups, you may also attract competition. Supposedly imitation is a form of flattery. But, it's annoying. You can't prevent this. In the worst cases, the competition gets intense and people become nasty and aggressive. Talk to the Chamber of Commerce or the Visitors' Bureau. Find out what your options are then exercise them. If things get out of hand, call the police.

Customer Caused Problems

The most unpredictable element of your tour is the customers. Generally, they are wonderful, friendly, attentive and polite. But occasionally, you get a bad apple. The basic principle in dealing with difficult customers is this: You cannot allow an individual or small group to ruin everyone else's experience. If you're not sure what to do, ask yourself what's best for the group as a whole and you'll know the right answer. Some people need to be booted. It's awkward and will make them unhappy. It will make everyone else ecstatic. Fortunately, this is a rare occurrence.

Disruptive customers come in lots of different shapes and sizes. There are know-it-alls, people who constantly interrupt, correct you, and ask endless tedious questions. And there are "helpful" folks who want to enhance everyone's experience by volunteering additional information, most of which is incorrect and all of which is boring. You need to shut these people down as quickly and nicely as you can.

Say something like, "We've got a lot of great material to cover this afternoon, but we'll never get through it if we don't stay on schedule. I want to respect everyone's time. So please hold your questions and comments until I finish my presentation at each stop. If you want to dig a little deeper, come up here and walk with me. We'll talk on the way."

The opposite problem is the silent, passive audience. They don't react to anything. They don't laugh, ask questions, nod, smile. And if they are teenagers, they don't even look at you. I've had groups like this and it is unnerving. The only thing you can do is to keep going, give the best tour you can and get to the end.

The lesson I've learned from passive, silent groups and individuals who look like they are having the worst time of their lives is that you really don't know what they're thinking.

I'll never forget one guy who seemed so miserable throughout the entire tour I finally stopped looking at him because it was starting to throw my presentation off. After the tour, he approached me. I figured he was going to ask for a refund. Instead he said he was a policeman and had really enjoyed the evening. He then spent about half an hour telling me some of the funniest stories I've ever heard about shenanigans in a local graveyard. His demeanor never changed.

Another example of not knowing what's going through people's heads comes from Ghost Trek. One evening people were wandering up, paying, milling around and waiting for the tour to start. I usually make small talk, ask them where they're from, that sort of thing. I started chatting with an older woman who was with her teenaged granddaughter. Suddenly, the woman pointed to the girl and said, "Her Daddy just died a couple of days ago." I don't know about you, but if one of my family members had just passed away, the last thing in the world I'd want to do is go on a ghost tour.

Don't make assumptions about why people leave the tour early. It happens. Don't worry about it. If most of your group peels off, you have a problem. That's not what I'm talking about. I'm talking about instances when one or two people drift away. Here are some common reasons that happens:

- They are bored.

- They would rather go into the bar we just passed than continue the walk.
- They need a bathroom.
- They are hungry.
- Their child is fussing or bored (we want them to leave in this case).
- It's too hot, too cold, raining, etc.
- They wore the wrong shoes. Really.

If people who leave the tour want their money back, give it to them. It's not worth arguing. Besides, you still have to conduct the rest of the tour for the remaining folks. If you have a helper, give him or her some cash and put them in charge of refunds.

There is also that special group of customers who fall into the "Just Plain Nuts" category. We had two ladies on Ghost Trek who became very angry when we refused to guarantee they would actually see ghosts on the tour. We couldn't say goodbye to them fast enough.

You can avoid several common problems by setting ground rules at the very beginning of the tour. Ask people to turn the ringers on their cell phones off. Nobody is going to turn their phone off completely so don't bother asking them to do that. Say something like, "It gets kind of noisy from time to time and I want to make sure everyone can hear. So please put your phones on vibrate. If you want to talk on the phone, go ahead, but step away from the group."

The same applies to smokers. Ask them to step away from the group if they're going to smoke. If you deal with this type of thing up front, no one is singled out. Everyone understands and 99.99% percent of people will comply.

Let everyone know if there are any restrictions on taking photos, videos or voice recordings. Almost everyone has a camera in their phone. Encourage your customers to take pictures. You want them to post on Facebook, Twitter and Instagram and talk about what fun they're having on your tour.

People on our tours have taken amazing photos which we've used – with their permission – over and over in our promotional material. If you've got a helper, have him or her take pictures of the group as the tour progresses. Have fun with this and let your audience have fun too. Don't impose unnecessary restrictions.

Having said all that, if there is a venue on the route that prohibits photography, you must respect that. Make sure your group understands and then emphasize when they can once again shoot at will.

Every once in a while, you'll pick up a straggler, someone who joins the tour midstream, someone you know has not paid. If you've got a helper, he or she can handle this. If you're working alone, don't interrupt your presentation. When you are ready to move on to the next stop, approach the person and say something like, "Hi. This is a tour about blah blah. Would you like to join us? It's $15."

Occasionally, especially when you have a massive group, there may be people on the fringes who don't pay. There's nothing you can do about this so don't worry about it. Most people are honest and will come up at the end and pay voluntarily.

Finally, you must be prepared for emergencies. Keep your own cell phone on, set on mute or vibrate. If someone falls, faints, gets sick or hurt, you'll be ready to call for help immediately. If you don't have a cell phone, get one.

Here's a checklist that will help you avoid several of the most likely problems, especially when you're just starting out.

Countdown to Tour Day Checklist

2- 3 days prior

- Contact everyone involved, guides, helpers, experts, owners of venues. Remind them about the upcoming tour and make sure they are still on board. If they are not, adjust as necessary.
- Prepare any handouts.
- Check costumes and props.
- Test all equipment.
- Start watching the weather.
- If you haven't already done so, prepare your notes.

1 day prior

- Check your sign.

- Make sure you have plenty of change in the right denominations.
- Go to the tour route and check for construction, roadblocks or other obstacles.
- What time do you plan to leave your house on tour day? Have you allowed enough travel time? Make sure the place you plan to park will work.
- Test your keys at the venue if you're responsible for opening.

Tour Day

- Dress for the weather.
- Don't forget your water.
- Don't forget your notes.
- Don't forget the change.
- If you are accepting credit/debit cards don't forget your processing device.
- Don't forget your microphone, flashlight, laser pointer, etc.
- Don't forget your phone and camera.
- Leave early enough.
- There's only one first time. Have fun!

Doomsday or No Big Deal?

Look at the following scenarios. Which would you rather deal with?

Scenario 1 - The big day finally arrived. The weather couldn't have been better. You got to the tour starting point early. You were prepared, excited and ready to go. And no one showed up. You're devastated. What went wrong?

Any number of things could have kept people away. It could have been a simple typo. The newspaper printed the wrong date or time. There was an error on a poster. You really should have caught the error, but typos do slip through.

Maybe you scheduled the tour at the wrong time of day or on a day of the week that just doesn't work for people. Did you pick a topic no one is interested in or one that's been covered so many times everyone is tired of it? Do people think the neighborhood where the tour was being offered is dangerous or beyond bland?

The most likely reason no one showed up is they didn't know about it. Your promotional efforts were inadequate, misdirected or both. You failed to reach your target audience or your description of the tour wasn't appealing enough. It's hard, if not impossible, to know exactly what went wrong if you've only made one attempt.

This undoubtedly feels like a disaster. But it's really not that big of a deal. You haven't lost any ground. Don't give up. It's time to fine-tune and adjust.

Scenario 2 - The big day finally arrived. The weather couldn't have been better. You got to the tour starting point early which was a good thing since there were about 100 people already waiting. Before it was all said and done, it seemed like the entire town had shown up. People sometimes refer to this as a good problem. They're wrong. This is a disaster.

Even though you had a helper, you were completely overwhelmed. You did manage to run the tour, but it was chaotic and went way over schedule. No one could hear. Most people were gone by about the half-way point. Those who stayed until the bitter end went away unhappy.

You obviously did a great job promoting the tour. But the product, the tour experience itself, fell short of expectations. You also need to fine-tune and adjust.

What Can Go Right?

Scenario 3 - The big day finally arrived. The weather couldn't have been better. You got to the tour starting point early. You were prepared, excited and ready to go. Twenty-four people showed up. You were a little nervous at first, but you found your stride and did it!

Your customers loved the tour so much they clapped at the end and wanted to know when you were going to offer it again. They said they wanted to come back and bring their friends.

And it's not just the customers who were happy. The tour was a success by your own definition whether that means you made a good profit, increased visibility for your organization or you are basking in a well-deserved sense of accomplishment. When things go well, it's so much fun.

Honestly, a positive outcome is much more likely than the disaster scenarios described above. Especially when you have taken the time to understand your audience, created a top-tier experience that exceeds their expectations, carefully planned it all out, checked and double checked the details and not left things to chance.

Regardless of how it went, congratulations for getting out there and doing it! We'll discuss how to make it better – and it absolutely will get better and easier – in the next chapter on Post-Tour Assessment.

Chapter 9 – Post-Tour Assessment

You did it! Even if the turnout was less than you'd hoped or things didn't go exactly as planned, you still deserve a huge pat on the back. It takes courage to put yourself out there. Good job.

If you are going to offer this tour over and over, it's just going to get better with time and practice. If it was a once only event, the next time you plan a tour, the entire process will be easier and faster. You've learned a lot.

It's time to reflect on your experience.

The Post-Mortem

The post-tour assessment process does not have to be elaborate. You just need to be honest with yourself and look for ways to improve your product.

Open your notebook or folder and turn to the beginning of Chapter 3 – Designing the Tour. You wrote a short paragraph, a general description of how you envisioned the tour at that point in the process. How closely did the final product match your early description? Were you way off or right on target? What are your general thoughts on the direction the tour process took?

Next do a quick write up of the factual details of the tour.

- How many people attended? How many adults, kids, seniors if you offered kids or seniors discounts?
- How much money did you take in?

Now consider things from a more subjective angle. Jot down the answers to the following questions as well as anything else that comes to mind. If you were not the guide, interview the person who was. If you had several people working on the tour, stationary hosts for example, talk to all of them. They have valuable information.

- Was this a larger or smaller turnout than you expected?
- Was there anything unusual about the day or evening? Bad weather? Competing event?
- Did people seem to enjoy the tour?
- Did you receive any specific compliments or complaints?
- Did anyone suggest changes? What were they?
- Did you enjoy working on the tour? Why or why not?

- What seemed to be people's favorite stop or tour element?
- What seemed to be people's least favorite stop or element?
- Did anything about how the tour proceeded surprise you?
- How did the timing work? Too short? Too long?
- How about the amount of walking? Was that OK for people?
- What was the smartest thing you did during the planning process?
- What was the worst thing you did?
- Did you miss anything important or skip a critical step?
- Was there something you thought people would love that bombed?
- Was there something you thought was so-so that they loved?
- If you had multiple people working on the tour, how did that go? Too many people? Not enough?

Audience Input

The best way to find out what people think about the tour is to ask them. The best time to do that is immediately after the event. People often come up afterwards and tell you they liked the tour or ask a question about a particular stop. Use the opportunity to get a little more information if you can.

If they say, "That was fun. I really liked the tour." Say something like, "I'm glad you liked it! What was your favorite part? What else do you think I should add to it?"

If they have questions, do your best to answer them. Then say something like, "What do you know about the old XYZ Building? What other places around here have good stories?"

Doing a written survey is next to impossible if you're walking around outside. What you can do, however, is to mention your website and Facebook page at the end of the tour. Tell people you're going to be posting some pictures. Invite them to visit online and share what they thought of the tour. Tell them you are interested in any suggestions they have. Hand out cards with your name, website, social addresses and contact information. You can make these very cheaply by getting sheets of business card blanks and printing them yourself.

I hope you were able to get input from your customers. Summarize what you learned in your notebook or folder.

If you want to use a written survey and that works in your situation, feel free to adapt the following to meet your needs. You could also add this to your website or send it to your newsletter subscribers.

Sample Survey

We are planning new programs and would like to know what interests you.

1. Which do you prefer?
- An open house type tour
- A walking tour with a guide
- An indoor sit-down presentation with slides and pictures
- Other – please tell us what
2. Would you be interested in an historic photo safari and/or scavenger hunt?
3. Would you be interested in a "Marietta Vice" tour that delved into the seedy side of our fair city's past?

4. What other topics would you like us to focus on? Do you have a suggestion for a new program, tour or event?

Enter your email to receive free program updates from Hidden Marietta.

Thanks for sharing your ideas!

Executive Summary

Now is the time to write an executive summary, three short paragraphs describing the tour and how everything went. Even if you are not required to do this for your board of directors, upper management or others, do the write up anyway.

The first paragraph is a description of the tour concept. You have already written that. It's in your notebook or folder. Use the second paragraph to provide attendance figures, costs, income and net profit or loss. The final paragraph is a summary and assessment for the future. Here are two examples of final paragraphs.

Example 1 – Hidden Places, Secret Spaces – History is part of Marietta's DNA. It is mentioned over and over by both out-of-town visitors and local people looking for new and different experiences. Our historic downtown is a key component in our larger story. The individual buildings and the aspects of the past they illuminate are largely unexplored territory. This popular, profitable, and easy to run program will provide excellent returns for years to come.

Example 2 – Harvest Home Tour – Although turnout was not huge, we were very pleased. This is a new tour and a new concept for Cambridge. The people who attended loved the event. They want to do it again and to bring their friends. Word-of-mouth should be a positive factor. The building owners who participated had positive experiences as well. All in all, this was an excellent community event and should only get bigger and better with time.

Fine-Tuning

It's time to think about how to improve your tour. Maybe you only need a few minor tweaks. Maybe you need an extreme makeover. Either way, as you contemplate the future, consider the following big picture questions.

- How can you improve things for your customers?
- How can you improve your bottom line?
- How can you improve things for your organization, your guides, helpers and volunteers?
- And perhaps most importantly, how can you improve things for yourself?

You've come a long way. Take credit for what you've accomplished. Above all, don't give up. Keep practicing. Keep coming up with new ideas. Keep listening to your customers and keep improving your product. I wish you the very best!

Author Information

My tourism career began in 1986 when I started as a front-line travel agent. Eventually, I worked my way up to ownership of a thriving commercial agency in the heart of Washington, DC. I've escorted tour groups, taught at a travel school and conducted dozens of destination workshops. I was the marketing director of a tour operator specializing in Southeast Asia, represented the China International Travel Service and managed all travel programs for ASTA, the world's largest travel trade association.

After moving to the small town of Marietta, Ohio, I immersed myself in the world of local history and hyper-local tourism. I founded my own tour company. My first program was a ghost walk. The tour was so popular, I attracted the attention of The History Press, a traditional publishing house. The two books I wrote for them – **Haunted Marietta: History and Mystery in Ohio's Oldest City** and **A Guide to**

Historic Marietta, Ohio – are available online and in bookstores nationwide.

The best part of my local history and tourism adventure was working with community groups. I collaborated with Main Street organizations, visitors' bureaus, county and state historical societies, a public library, downtown merchants' associations, hotels, restaurants, a college, a community theater and several attractions including historic houses, museums and even an old-fashioned riverboat. You'll find lots of local history tour and program ideas and other free resources at TheHistoryBiz.com.

I now live in Albuquerque, New Mexico and I'm excited to share the amazing things I'm learning about this beautiful state on my New Mexico history and travel blog. It's at HiddenNewMexico.com. You can keep up with everything else I'm doing at LynneSturtevant.com.

Thanks again for reading **Create Successful Walking Tours**. Do you have questions about the material? Was there a section or sections that weren't clear? Is there an area you'd like information (or more information) on? Feel free to contact me at Lpsturtevant@gmail.com or via the contact pages on any of my websites. I'd love to hear from you.

Books

Explore the world of local history and travel with Lynne Sturtevant. All titles are available on Amazon.

The Collaboration Kit

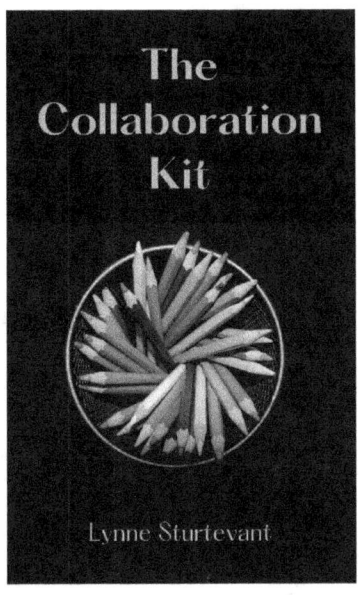

Collaboration can be the easiest, most effective and least expensive way to quickly produce new programs, tours and events – but only if you work with the right partner.

The Collaboration Kit is a practical, how-to guide written specifically for people working in local history and tourism.

Topics include the benefits of collaborating, how to find and approach potential partners, what to do if you're approached, why to consider working with competitors, red flags, and program examples and suggestions.

There are also four real world case studies including a detailed analysis of a single doomed program that went off the rails twice with two different partners. There's even a sample collaboration agreement you can adopt and adapt to your own situation.

A Guide to Historic Marietta, Ohio

Welcome to Marietta, the elegant river city where Ohio's history begins. Explore ancient earthworks, stroll shady brick streets lined with glorious Victorian mansions, wander through museums, browse for antiques in the beautifully preserved downtown, kickback in a wide variety of restaurants and taverns or take a relaxing cruise down the scenic Ohio River. Venture into nearby West Virginia and visit Fenton, America's oldest art glass company; Blennerhassett Island where Aaron Burr hatched a plot against the US government; and Henderson Hall, the majestic great house of a former slave plantation – all within

15 miles of downtown Marietta. **A Guide to Historic Marietta, Ohio** will help you make the most of your time. It includes an overview of the area's rich history, maps, dozens of vintage and modern photos and descriptions of the best sites and attractions the region has to offer – including those most visitors miss.

Haunted Marietta: History and Mystery in Ohio's Oldest City

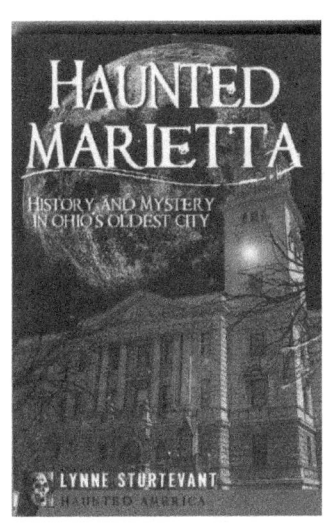

Haunted Marietta: History and Mystery in Ohio's Oldest City explores the supernatural side of the state's first settlement. Visit a crumbling 1835 mansion whose original owner still roams the halls, sit in the plush red seats of an abandoned theater and climb an ancient Indian burial mound. Encounter river pirates, fugitive slaves, an axe murderer, jealous lovers and inept morticians. ***Haunted Marietta*** delves into various types of otherworldly phenomena, examines the difference between ghost stories and reports of supernatural activity and discusses why certain people become spirits. From an 1815 goblin sighting to a bartender's brush with the unexplained, local author Lynne Sturtevant covers it all.

Hometown: Writing a Local History or Travel Guide

Many of us dream of becoming published authors. We imagine how it would feel to hold our own book or see it on the shelf at our favorite bookstore. The good news is you can achieve your dream by writing about your hometown.

You can chronicle your area's history. Write about a significant building or local celebrity. Zero in on an interesting neighborhood or time period. Publish a collection of ghost stories or share insider tips and recommendations in a travel book about your town or region.

Hometown: Writing a Local History or Travel Guide is a complete guide to writing and publishing a local interest book.

Topics include choosing the right subject, scope and slant for your book; structuring your project so that you actually finish the manuscript; an honest comparison of traditional and self-publishing options; step-by-step instructions for publishing on Amazon; specific ways to capitalize on local authors' inherent marketing advantages; how to establish your online presence; and how much you might realistically earn in your book's first year and beyond.

www.ingramcontent.com/pod-product-compliance
Lightning Source LLC
Chambersburg PA
CBHW060847220526
45466CB00003B/1274